Can I change your mind.

The craft and art of persuasive writing

Lindsay Camp

A & C Black • London

D0308368

First published in Great Britain 2007

A & C Black Publishers Ltd
38 Soho Square, London W1D 3HB

© Lindsay Camp 2007

A CIP record for this book is available from
the British Library.

ISBN-10: 0-7136-7849-6
ISBN-13: 978-0-7136-7849-9

This book is produced using paper that is made from
wood grown in managed, sustainable forests. It is
natural, renewable and recyclable. The logging and
manufacturing processes conform to the environmental
regulations of the country of origin.

Design by Fiona Pike, Pike Design, Winchester
Typeset in 10/14pt New Baskerville and 9/14 Univers 45
Printed in the United Kingdom by Bookmarque

For my friend and mentor, David Stuart.

And in memory of my highly persuasive father.

Contents

Thank you

My warmest thanks to Jeremy Bullmore, whose writings have inspired me and whose ideas about how communication works I have shamelessly borrowed in this book.

Many thanks also to Lisa Carden and Nicky Thompson for believing people might be interested in persuasive writing and for eagle-eyed attention to detail, respectively.

And thanks, finally, for keeping me out of trouble, to my lawyer, Anna Keeling (who also has the misfortune to be my wife).

I'd like to thank the following for the use of extracts reproduced in this book. The Lonely Hearts ad on page 66 is taken from *They Call Me Naughty Lola – the London Review of Books personal ads: a reader*, edited by David Rose and published by Profile Books 2006. Copyright belongs to London Review of Books.

The example of Jeremy Bullmore's writing is reproduced from *Campaign* magazine with the permission of the copyright owner, Haymarket Business Publications Limited.

'The Six Rules for Good Writing' are reprinted from *Politics and the English Language* by George Orwell (Copyright © George Orwell, 1946) by permission of Bill Hamilton as the Literary Executor of the Estate of the Late Sonia Brownell Orwell and Secker & Warburg Ltd.

Section One
Persuasive principles

Chapter 1
Persuasive writing – who needs it?

Why Lily is to blame for me writing this book; what I mean by persuasive writing, and why it's a skill that can be useful to just about anyone, both at work and in real life; and finally, a bit about what I write for a living, and why it might be relevant to you.

One day, a couple of years ago, I asked my daughter – who was seven at the time – what she'd been doing at school. If you have children, you'll know how rarely this question receives a satisfactory answer. So imagine my surprise when she replied 'persuasive writing'.

Persuasive writing! When I was that age, as far as I can remember, my school days were spent colouring in, collecting interesting twigs for the nature table and gasping at the incident-packed adventures of Janet and John. It was one of those moments when a parent realises just what a different world his kids are growing up in. But, more to the point, it was the moment when it first really struck me that my painfully acquired professional skills might have a wider usefulness than I had ever previously imagined.

Actually, that isn't quite true. I had, I suppose, always been vaguely aware that the basic principles which govern the kind of writing I do for a living could, and should, be applied to many other types of written communication. But what that brief conversation with Lily brought home to me was the fact that the rest of the world was starting to cotton on; to understand that the ability to argue a case effectively in writing isn't just a handy accomplishment – like being able to change a fuse or fold a napkin into a crown – but a basic life-skill.

Put simply, if seven-year-olds all over Britain are learning to write persuasively, it's time everyone did.

What exactly do I mean by persuasive writing?

Before we go any further, I think we need to be as clear as possible about the subject under discussion, and how it might be relevant to you. So what, specifically, is it that distinguishes persuasive writing from other kinds of writing? My answer – and I hope Lily's teacher would agree – is that:

> In persuasive writing, the main purpose is to influence the way a reader thinks, feels or acts.

Let's try to pin it down further by listing 10 examples of persuasive writing, as defined above:

- Your CV
- Any kind of proposal or fund-raising document

- An email to your biggest client, tactfully pointing out that unless your invoice is settled promptly, your company might be compelled to take appropriate measures
- Recruitment materials of any kind
- A letter to your bank, explaining why you need a bigger overdraft
- A memo to your staff, suggesting they might like to give up their Sunday afternoon to take part in a charity event
- Any press release
- Your performance appraisal form, explaining to your boss why you deserve a big pay rise
- The flyer for the PTA promises auction – only two weeks left, and all you have so far is an evening's baby-sitting and one free dental inspection
- Any invitation

Anything there that rings a bell with you? I hope so; but not to worry if there isn't. My aim, at this stage, is just to impress upon you that you don't need to be planning a career in advertising, marketing or PR to benefit from reading this book. The principles and skills that I am going to talk about can, to a greater or lesser extent, be applied to virtually anything you will ever need to write.

An exaggerated claim? I hope not, since good persuasive writers have no truck with hyperbole; but to justify my contention, we may need to broaden our terms of reference a little.

An introduction to 'semi-persuasive' writing

Of course, it's true that the examples I chose above are the types of writing task which most closely resemble the work produced by a professional copywriter. What is your CV, after all, if it isn't an advertisement selling what you have to offer to a potential employer? But let's consider some other types of writing which, at first glance, may seem to have little or nothing to do with persuasion.

Any suggestions? Well, how about an email replying to a colleague who has asked for some information; a contact report on a meeting with a client; oh yes, and a school history essay. Obviously, in none of these three cases is the writer's main purpose to influence how the reader feels, thinks or acts. But equally obviously, whatever prompts a writer to write, the result may well influence the reader – although the effect may be slight or imperceptible in many cases. Will the colleague receiving the email be satisfied with the information supplied? Will the client respond positively to the summary of what took place at the meeting? And will the teacher marking the essay be impressed not just by its content, but by the effort that has gone into it?

Looked at in this light, virtually everything we write has a 'persuasive' aspect to it: the capacity to influence, either positively or negatively, the person (or people) who will be reading it.

But is it Art? (If so, wrong book I'm afraid)

So is there any kind of writing which can't, in this very loose sense, be considered 'persuasive'? Yes, I think there is. For me, true creative writing – Writing as Art, if you like – comes from a completely different place, where completely different rules apply. And the most important of these, I believe, is that genuine artists should be driven by the desire for self-expression.

This doesn't mean, of course, that they don't care about how people respond to their work. But what it does mean is that they can never let this dictate to them. Artists must always give absolute priority to finding the best possible way of giving shape and substance to their own vision, regardless of whether that makes it more or less 'accessible' to the general public; easier or harder to understand. A real creative writer would never change a single comma just to please the reader.

As persuasive writers, on the other hand, we're perfectly happy to tweak our punctuation – and do much more besides – if it makes our reader more likely to respond in the way that we want.

Persuasive writing: the same principles always apply

I hope you won't mind if I close this first chapter by telling you a little more about myself – not because I'm hoping to dazzle you with my professional achievements

Who needs persuasive writing? Just ask your local hereditary peer.

So, it's 1999 and you are a lord. You're minding your own business, happily passing your days oppressing the peasantry or killing things on your grouse moor, when that nasty oikish Blair fellow announces that he's planning to abolish you.

Well, what he actually announces is that almost all hereditary peers are to be booted out of the House of Lords. Only 92 out of a total of over 750 will be permitted to retain their membership of the best gentlemen's club in town. And if you think you ought to be one of those happy few, you should write a 75-word manifesto explaining why. What are you going to write? If you're the late Lord Monckton of Brenchley, you get out your fountain pen, fill it with green ink and scribble:

I support:

The Queen and all the Royal Family.

The United Kingdom and not a Disunited Republic.

Action against cruelty to animals, particularly fishing with rods. All cats to be muzzled outside to stop the agonising torture of mice and small birds.

The police must be supported against the increase in violent crime.

Organic food not GM.

There should be more grammar schools not less.

LEVEL UP not level down. God willing.

> And then, having presented such a compelling case to your peers, you wonder why you weren't elected. More proof, if needed, that these days nobody – noble or commoner – can predict when basic persuasive writing skills will come in handy.

or make you gasp with envy at my glamorous lifestyle, but because I want to establish as clearly as I can, from the outset, how the things I write for a living are relevant to the things you may need to write.

I started my career as a trainee copywriter at J Walter Thompson, then the biggest advertising agency in the UK. Arriving quite rapidly at the recognition that I was too good and kind for the ruthless cut and thrust of ad agency life, I fled from London and started working as a freelance.

That, terrifyingly, was nearly 25 years ago – since when I have written virtually everything it's possible to be paid for writing. A slight exaggeration maybe; but, to give you some impression of the diversity of the work I do, let me list, pretty much at random, a few of my fairly recent assignments:

- A website for a big commercial law firm
- A speech about the need for radical change in the design industry
- An annual report for a well-known high street retailer
- A label for a champagne bottle to be presented by a firm of estate agents to their clients on moving day

- A fund-raising newsletter for a young people's charity
- A set of 'brand language' guidelines for a major financial institution

As I said, I'm not trying to impress you. My point is that the one constant in my professional output is the need to persuade. The main purpose of everything I write is to influence the way a reader thinks, feels or acts. Of course, writing a couple of short sentences to appear on a champagne label is different from writing a 10,000-word annual report. But I firmly believe that, in both cases – and in everything I'm paid to write – the basic principles of persuasive communication apply.

And, thanks in part to Lily, I have come to believe that they can be successfully applied much more widely still.

Remember that entertaining TV commercial you saw last night? That website where you booked your last holiday? Even that mailshot you received this morning and chucked straight in the bin? They all have something to teach you about how you could be a better, more persuasive writer.

Chapter 2
The three Rs of good persuasive writing

A brief introduction to the Big Theory that this book is based upon, summed up in the snappy slogan, 'Remember the Reader and the Result'; a hypothetical caravan-related example of where this theory leads us; and the famous Indian Wood Carver analogy.

In a moment, I'm going to tell you my Big Theory about persuasive writing. But first, I'm going to tell you my Big Theory about Big Theories. It's that books which appear to be based on a Big Theory usually aren't. In most cases, they are based on quite a small theory, which may amount to little more than a fairly obvious statement of a common-sensical point of view.

I'll give you a couple of examples. Those management tomes that sell in their thousands in departure lounge book stalls around the world. All, as far as I am aware, could be summarised in a dozen or so words: 'Be nice to people, treat them well, and they will work harder and more productively'; or, of course, the opposite: 'Be nasty to people, treat them mean, make them fear for their jobs, and they will work harder and more productively.' Or how about diet books? Here's the Lindsay Camp Way to a Healthier Slimmer You in just six words, one of them not strictly necessary:

Eat less, take more exercise, dummy!

If we were being cynical, we might conclude from this that the authors of books based upon Big Theories are rogues and charlatans, intent on defrauding gullible readers; that their only skill lies in taking a self-evident commonsensical point and teasing and stretching it to fill a fat tome.

But instead, let's put this more charitable interpretation on my Big Theory about Big Theories: that, in almost every field of human activity, the basic principles of what works, and what doesn't, are pretty self-evident and commonsensical; but, in the hurly burly of everyday life, people tend to lose sight of them, and simple truths become obscured. So the writers of those Big Theory-based books aren't attempting to pull the wool over anyone's eyes, but to remove the scales; to show their readers something that may once have been familiar in a fresh light; to strip away complexities that have built up around a subject over time, and reveal the surprisingly simple truth.

Anyway, that's my justification for the fact that I could easily distil all the wit and wisdom I have to offer you on good persuasive writing into one not particularly long sentence. Here goes:

My Big Theory about Persuasive Writing

The secret of good persuasive writing is to be as clear as you possibly can be about two things: who your reader is, and what result you are hoping to achieve.

In fact, I could even encapsulate it in a snappy six-word slogan, which I'm tempted to call the Three Rs of Persuasive Writing:

Remember the Reader and the Result.

Or, perhaps, just RRR.

A very rough indication of what RRR means in practice

We'll get down to details later. But let me give you the merest hint of where this Big Theory leads us. Let's imagine that you have a caravan that you really love, but which financial necessity compels you to sell. (Not entirely plausible, I know, but bear with me.) You decide to put a postcard in the window of your local corner shop. You sit down to write. And, because you love your caravan so much, what you write is a poem about the last, wonderful holiday you had in it. The only problem is that the poem turns out rather long, so that you have to write it very small indeed on the postcard, and there isn't room for any tedious details about what type of caravan it is, how many it sleeps, what kind of floor coverings and kitchen appliances it features, and so on.

The milkman's note test

The best thing I've written recently? Without hesitation, I'd say it was the note I wrote to the milkman a couple of nights ago, which I'm now going to reproduce in full:

'No milk today thanks, Dave!'

I'm serious. Just consider how effective it was. When I came down next morning, bleary-eyed, there on my doorstep was ... nothing. No milk at all. Not a single bottle. My note had been 100% successful in achieving its objective.

Why? Two reasons. First, because I knew when I wrote it precisely what that objective was. And second, because I had a very clear picture of my reader in my mind before I started.

Worth bearing in mind next time you write something that doesn't read quite as persuasively as you'd like.

You've forgotten your reader, haven't you? How is anyone supposed to buy your beloved caravan if they don't know anything about it?

Luckily, you realise this in time, and rewrite the postcard, including all the information that somebody looking for a caravan might want, as well as a nice picture of you and your family having a lovely time on holiday in the Brecon Beacons. It's much better. Except that this time you forget to put your phone number at the bottom. So, while you may have many potential buyers ready to outbid each other for your caravan, they have no way of contacting you.

You've forgotten the result you're trying to achieve.

Of course, you wouldn't be foolish enough to do any of the above. But my Big Theory is based on the observation that many intelligent people – including you, perhaps – do indeed make mistakes similar in kind, if not in degree of stupidity, every time they sit down to write[1].

---

[1]I was worried when I wrote this that the hypothetical example was too far removed from reality to be enlightening. Then, a few weeks later, somebody put one of those take-away menus through my letterbox. Delicious-sounding Moroccan food, tempting prices, prompt home delivery … no phone number or address.

The Indian Wood Carver Analogy

My friends at The Chase, perhaps the UK's wittiest graphic design consultancy, used to tell a story about an old Indian craftsman who spent his days carving beautiful elephants from blocks of wood. When asked how he did it, he would reply, 'I just cut away the wood that doesn't look like an elephant.'

The designers at The Chase believed this story illuminated their craft, as carvers of beautifully fashioned communications. They were right. But it also illustrates how my Big Theory can help us be better persuasive writers in practice: all we have to do to create a masterpiece is cut away everything that, bearing in mind who our reader is, won't help us achieve the result we want.

Which should leave us with a perfect elephant.

Chapter 3
Understanding your reader

Some preliminary observations about how readers actually read, and what the implications are for persuasive writers; then pages and pages about how to build up an accurate picture of the specific individual reader – the 'audience of one' – you will be addressing in a particular piece of writing; finally, a very little bit about you, the reader of this book.

I'd like you to think about the last thing you read. It doesn't really matter what it was, provided it was more than a couple of paragraphs long. A seed catalogue, maybe. The latest issue of *Hello!* A market research report. The last chapter of this book. Whatever it was, I'd like you to cast your mind back to when you read it, and then answer the following questions:

1 Did you start at the beginning and read straight through to the end?
2 Did you read every word?
3 Did you believe and/or agree with every word?

Bad writers worry about whether the reader will understand them. Good ones are more concerned about how well they understand the reader.

I'd be willing to bet that you answered no to at least one of those questions, and quite possibly all three. What makes me so sure? Well, I may have been a professional writer since the days of quill pens and parchment, but I've been a reader for even longer. I've observed other people reading, too. I've even read the odd learned article about how people read. All of which qualifies me, I think, to make a few sweeping generalisations on the subject.

What do we know about readers, in general?

As persuasive writers, we can broadly make the following assumptions about the reader we are addressing. She[2]:

- has better things to do
- never reads from start to finish
- always reads between the lines
- is not an idiot

I'd like to expand a bit on each of these observations ...

---

[2]Throughout this book, I'll be referring to 'the reader', in the singular. I don't like the convention of using the plural pronoun 'they' in such cases; and 'he or she' is bound to get clumsy. So I've made a somewhat arbitrary decision to assign female gender to 'the reader' whenever she makes an appearance.

The reader has better things to do

Uncontroversial, this, I think. We live, it's widely agreed, in a fast-paced world where most people have too much to do, too little time and far, far too much information coming at them from every direction. Creative writers may hope, sometimes justifiably, that their readers will happily clear a space in their busy schedules to snuggle down with a good book. But persuasive writing is different; it has to compete for the reader's attention – and not just to gain it in the first place, but also to hold it. Good persuasive writing gives the reader a compelling reason to read and to continue reading.

The reader never reads from start to finish

Observe yourself, or watch other people reading on the train, and you will see that reading is never an uninterrupted, 'linear' process. When we read, our eyes constantly scan the page – flickering over pictures, headings and other highlighted text, glancing ahead, going back to check what we've already read, jumping to the final paragraph. What we're doing, of course, is assessing whether it's worth continuing to read. Not just once or twice, but repeatedly, we're asking ourselves the question, 'How long will it take me to extract what I want from this – and will I get enough from it to justify the time it takes?'

In the next chapter I'll be considering the importance of knowing what your objective is when you write. But it's worth pausing here to note that readers have objectives, too; in particular, the desire to gain something of value in return for their investment of time.

The reader always reads between the lines

I'm planning to say a lot about this, which may well be the most important point in the book, so I'll keep it brief for now. But it's vital to establish that, when we read, we never take the words on the page in front of us at face value. We don't simply absorb from them the information or ideas that the writer wanted to convey. We interpret them; we look for hidden meanings and secret agendas; we test them against our own understanding of the world. It's as if there is a little voice inside our heads, commenting on what we are reading. Some of the comments the little voice inside my head makes most frequently would be things like:

'Yeah, right.'

'Hmm, wonder what he means by that?'

'She's just contradicted herself, right there.'

'Pah! Phooey!'

'What was this guy on when he wrote this?'

And so on. Maybe your little voice is more polite. But the principle is the same: all readers always conduct a dialogue with themselves about what they are reading. (You're doing it now, aren't you? You're thinking: 'Is he right about that? Do I conduct a dialogue with myself when I'm reading?')

The reader is not an idiot

Good persuasive writing is not, repeat not, about trying to dupe, con or otherwise hoodwink the reader. You may sometimes be able to get away with lies and deceit, but in my view the risk is much too great. If the reader sees through you, your chances of establishing a rapport and building a relationship of trust are less than zero.

An only marginally less disastrous mistake is to show that you hold the reader's intelligence in contempt. Talk down to people, laboriously explain what they already know, make unwarranted assumptions about what their interests and priorities are, and you'll never win them over to your point of view. True, your reader may lack knowledge, but you should always assume that she possesses intelligence.

I wonder if the four observations above sound like the kind of statements of the obvious I was talking about in the last chapter? Perhaps they do. But, in that case, I have a question for you:

Why is it that when people write, they so often seem to forget completely what it's like to read?

How popele raed: the letsat thkiinng

I epxcet yu'voe seen taht tihng taht rlecetny did the rdnous on the itnernet abuot the way that radeers rogecnsie wrdos form teihr oevrlal saphe, rthaer tahn by selpling out all the idindvaul ltteers.

Itnreesintg, wsna't it? And good nwes, I gseus, for ayonne wohse sllpineg tndes to be a bit dgody.

But how is tihs rvelenat to us as prsauevise wiretrs? Hmmmm, not srue. But I'd say taht aythnnig wihch meaks us pusae and tinhk aoubt how raderes ralely raed – as opopsed to how we wulod lkie tehm to raed – has to be a good tihng.

What do we know about this specific reader?

I suppose there may be the occasional exception – the odd reader who actually, with the best will in the world, *is* an idiot – but broadly, everything I've said so far about how people read applies across the board when we write persuasively. But what about the specific reader we are addressing in a particular piece of writing? What can we say with any confidence about her?

In some cases, a great deal. I'm thinking of situations where the intended recipient of whatever we're writing is someone we know – a friend, family member, colleague, fellow steam locomotive enthusiast, or whatever. If we know the person who will be our reader, of course, we start with an enormous advantage: the ability to 'personalise' the communication. And the better we know them, the greater that advantage.

Personalising the message

At its crudest – when we know who the specific reader is, but very little else about her – personalisation may mean no more than starting a letter 'Dear Ms Taylor' rather than 'Dear Sir/Madam'. This gives us a head start in terms of striking up a relationship with the reader, but only a very small one. (It's also worth noting that, if we know next to nothing about the reader, attempts at personalisation can actually be counter-productive. It always makes me laugh, for example, when I receive those junk mail communications saying things like, 'Just imagine a brand new Peugeot 206 parked right outside 3rd Floor Flat, 203 Acacia Drive, Mr L Camp. And imagine all your friends saying, 'Wow, Mr L Camp has got a stunning new car ...')

But, as our level of acquaintance with the reader rises, so our ability to write something highly personalised – and persuasive – increases. Perhaps, for example, your boss has asked you for a note explaining why a pet project of yours deserves funding. You know your boss well. You know that she has three other projects to consider. You know that she's under pressure from the Board to achieve certain key strategic objectives. You know that she hates bullet points. So you write your report in such a way that it ever so politely rubbishes the three competing projects; demonstrates how your project fits perfectly with the company's key strategic objectives; and contains absolutely no bullet points. Your project gets the funding.

Of course, when we're writing (or, for that matter, talking) to somebody we know well, this kind of personalisation comes naturally. We automatically take into account our knowledge of that person – their interests and tastes; how much they know about the subject in question; their sense of humour (if any); their likely response, based on our previous experience of them – in shaping our communication with them.

But it all gets a lot more difficult when the need arises to address a wider audience. If you don't know your readers, how can you hope to make what you have to say relevant and engaging to them?

I'll do my best to answer this in a moment; but first, I'd like to persuade you that, however many people will read a piece of writing, it's always best to write as if you have …

… an audience of one

By which I mean that, in my book, good writing always addresses each reader as an individual, not as a member of a crowd.

In practical terms, this may not appear to make an enormous difference. All it means is using the singular 'you' when talking to the reader, rather than the plural. Here's an example of what I'm talking about from today's paper:

This episode is so bizarre that, without photographic evidence, I feel sure that the majority of you will think I've made it up.

That phrase 'the majority of you' stops me in my tracks. What does the writer mean? The majority of who? Or is he, perhaps, referring to the fact that we all of us contain multitudes; and that, while a small number of my multiple selves may be inclined to believe him, the 'majority of me' will probably be sceptical? Whatever the reason, I would very much rather have been addressed directly, one to one:

This episode is so bizarre that, without photographic evidence, I feel sure you will think I've made it up.

That may sound like a niggly, nit-picking little point. But I don't think it is. Reading is (almost always) a solitary activity. It happens inside your head; and when you read something that I've written, you are, in effect, allowing me to join you in there. I'm a guest. And as such, though I may know next to nothing about you, it's up to me to strike up a relationship with you; to find a way of making whatever I have to say engaging, stimulating and persuasive to you.

Getting to know the Unknown Reader

In the advertising business, we don't have the luxury of being on first names terms with the reader. Well, actually, that's not strictly true: if I write an ad, it's perfectly possible that my best mate Roger will see it in the newspaper. But I'm sure you get my point, which is that, since advertising reaches its target audience through mass media, it's always in the business of button-holing nameless strangers.

Yet good advertising invariably 'knows' the people it's talking to very well indeed.

How is this possible? In part, the answer lies in that jargon-y phrase, target audience. The best ads are nearly always those that are most accurately aimed. Clients – the people with something to sell, who pay for advertising – usually want their ads to address the widest possible audience. Agencies – the people who produce the ads for them – know that the narrower the audience, the easier it will be to find a really motivating way of talking to them. In a nutshell, the client is firmly convinced that his product is universally relevant to modern lifestyles; the agency, meanwhile, feels it will have a better chance of selling nasal hair-clippers to grooming-conscious older men.

So the first lesson that any persuasive writer can learn from advertising is the importance of narrowing down the target audience. True, the piece you are writing may be read by all kinds of different people; but the clearer you can be about what kind of person is most likely to 'buy' whatever it is you are 'selling', the greater your chances of success will be.

The aim, put simply, is to make writing for a reader you've never met as similar as possible to writing for one you know well.

Building up a picture of the reader

Back, briefly, to those nasal hair-clippers. Once the agency has won the argument with the client, and the decision has been taken to target men over 50, there are all kinds of sources of information available that can help to build up a picture of the kind of individual the advertising needs to address.

The agency can find out, from vast databases, how many men in the relevant age group regularly buy grooming products, or read *Private Eye*, or play golf, or have sex more than twice a month (and maybe even who with; I'm not quite sure how comprehensive the databases are). They might commission their own research, too – to find out how sufferers from nasal hirsutism feel about their affliction, or what remedies they have tried, or whether they like Joanna Lumley.

All the information thus obtained may, if used intelligently, help the agency to produce advertising that communicates effectively with the target audience.

Needless to say, you're not going to conduct a similarly exhaustive research and information-gathering exercise next time you write a new business mailshot, or whatever. But you can, and should, take the time, before you start writing, to list – or, at least make a mental note of – everything you know about the kind of individual who will be your reader.

Getting to know your reader: making intelligent assumptions

Of course, depending what you're writing, you may have access to little or no factual information about your reader. You may not even be sure whether he (or she) is male or female, young or old. So, in many cases, this stage of the persuasive writing process is not really a matter of gathering information, but of making reasonable assumptions. (If, for example, you decided to sell your compact studio flat by means of a classified ad in the local paper, you could reasonably assume that your reader was young and a first-time buyer.)

But, in any case, in my view factual information about the reader is over-rated. Knowing, for example, that I'm writing for a target audience of 'ABC1 males, aged 35–44', hardly helps me at all in attempting to find something engaging and motivating to say to them. No, the really important question for good persuasive readers isn't who the reader is, but what the reader is like.

So what is the reader like? A case for Sherlock Holmes

It might help to think of this as a piece of detective work; a process of deduction and elimination that should enable the writer to piece together a plausible 'photo-fit' picture of an elusive individual, the reader in question. Here are some of the leads we need to follow:

Why is the reader reading?

Broadly, we already know the answer to this: a piece of persuasive writing will be read if – and only if – the reader believes that she will get something of value in return for her investment of time. But that calculation which every reader makes ('Is it worth my while to read this?') may be based on a number of different factors; and I think there are three main 'sub-questions' which will determine the reader's decision.

1 'Is this useful/relevant to me?'

Sometimes, especially at work, people read because they know that a piece of writing contains information that is important or useful to them. They plough through dull documents for purely professional reasons. And, of course, this kind of 'need to know' reading doesn't only happen at the office. If you've ever flicked through a catalogue or scanned the local paper's classified columns, you were probably reading solely for the purpose of extracting information that you believed would be useful to you.

Refresca!

I'm on the train, and I'm pissed off again. We've just heard a short customer announcement in which our Train Manager referred not once, not twice, but three times to 'the Refresca café bar'.

Why should I care that it's called that? Why should I be remotely interested that the train operator has given its crappy on-board catering facilities a crappy brand name? No reason at all. It's their agenda, not mine. They're telling me something they want me to know, not something that I might conceivably find interesting, enjoyable or useful.

They're cluttering up a corner of my precious mental space with their verbal rubbish, and it's really, really annoying me.

Tell your reader what you want to say – rather than what they might be interested to hear – and you'll get much the same reaction.

If we have information which we have good reason to believe our reader will find useful, our duty is to write in such a way that nothing obscures or over-complicates it.

2 'How interesting is this?'

Of course, when we write persuasively, it's up to us to make the story we have to tell as gripping as possible, whatever it may be. But what I'm mainly concerned with here is the importance of gauging, before we start to write, our reader's existing level of interest in the subject. This will make a huge difference to what – and especially how much – we write.

At one time, for example, I used to work for a motor oil manufacturer. Nobody, I was firmly convinced, could possibly find motor oil interesting. And, most of the time, I was right: all the average motorist wanted to know was that Motor Oil X would stop his engine from seizing up, and was no more expensive than Brands Y and Z. But, occasionally, I was asked to write about mind-bogglingly expensive synthetic lubricants for an audience of high-performance car enthusiasts. And yes, incredibly, these were people who found lubrication fascinating; so much so that they genuinely wanted me to explain, in detail, how each individual molecule was chemically engineered, in order to provide maximum protection at engine temperatures up to 600°C and speeds in excess of 7000 rpm. So for this audience, I could easily get away with writing several hundred words, whereas the average Ford Fiesta driver would have dozed off after 25.

3 'Am I enjoying this?'
Of course, for persuasive writers entertaining the reader is never the primary aim. But we should always remember that – unless we're armed to the teeth with 'need to know' information or massively compelling arguments – we need to do everything we can to make reading as pleasurable as possible.

Think of beer advertising. Nobody would seriously suggest that one mass-market lager tastes different from another (especially after the first five pints). Give or take the odd widget, there are no serious competitive claims to be made in this market. So, from demonstrating how one lager refreshes the parts other beers can't reach to showing us a group of loveable men-children sticking out their tongues and saying 'Wasssup?' to each other, beer advertising has always relied almost entirely on entertainment value.

How relevant is this to the kind of persuasive writing that you might be doing? More than you might think. Because, in virtually any situation, the person who presents their case most engagingly will – all other things being equal – always have the edge. Which is why, like the host at a party, good persuasive writers make it their business to ensure that everyone is enjoying themselves.

The Useful/Interesting/Enjoyable equation

Perhaps if we were mathematically minded, we might be able to devise a formula that would help us here; a way of calibrating the three main reasons why readers read against each other, in order to calculate what quantity of each ingredient we need to make a specific communication work. Sadly, we most emphatically are not (mathematically minded, that is); but at least we can recognise that a kind of sliding scale works here – that the more Useful our writing is, the less Interesting it needs to be; the surer we are that what we are saying is of real and immediate Interest to our reader, the less cause we have to worry about how Enjoyable it is.

So much for why the reader is reading. The next big question is:

When is the reader reading?

Remember the note I wrote to the milkman? That's OK, you probably weren't expecting to be tested. Here it is again:

No milk today, thanks Dave!

I want you to take note of that word 'today'. You see, I was writing the note late one evening before going to bed, so the day when I wanted no milk was actually 'tomorrow'. But, because I knew that Dave wouldn't read my note until early the following morning, I wrote 'today'. Brilliant, eh? No, not really. But it's a point worth making that it pays for persuasive writers to think about when the reader will be reading. By this, I don't necessarily mean, literally, what time of day it will be. I'm referring more generally to the timing of the communication; whether a piece of writing reaches the reader when she is completely 'cold'; just starting to take an interest in the subject; or actively seeking information about it.

To understand the difference this makes, let's look briefly at the business of selling cars. To begin with, car manufacturers need to 'raise brand awareness'; that's to say, get themselves on a potential customer's shopping list. They do this by producing epic TV commercials, almost invariably featuring sweeping helicopter shots of the car in question traversing mountain passes to the accompaniment of pounding yet mellow rock music, frequently by Fleetwood Mac. The objective here is medium to long term: the viewer watching this extravaganza may well be a year or two from buying a new car, so the aim of the advertising is merely to plant a seed.

Look in your local paper, however, and you'll see a very different kind of advertising. Small, usually black and white ads packed with big prices, 0% finance offers, unrepeatable reductions and invitations to family fun days. These ads, produced by local car dealers, are aimed at car-buyers with money burning a hole in their pockets; people who are weeks or even just days away from driving the car of their dreams off the forecourt. Here the communication is time-critical – if the dealer doesn't get his message across now, he may well lose a sale.

Then, further down the road again, come the communications that dealers send to their existing customers, informing them of a new range of accessories or trying to persuade them to bring their cars in more regularly for servicing. This is 'aftersales marketing'; the process by which retailers attempt to maintain a profitable relationship with their customers, that will ultimately result in the customer returning to buy six more cars from them over the next 20 years.

Each of these different types of communication is actually addressing the same individual – but at different times in what we might call the buying cycle. When you write persuasively, you may not have an unrepeatable part-exchange deal to offer or a revolutionary new engine management system, but you can and should take into account when your words will reach your reader; what stage she will have reached in terms of her readiness to buy your argument. Is what you're saying completely new to her? Is she already showing an active interest, metaphorically poised with her money in her hand? Or is she an existing customer; someone who has already made a commitment – and may therefore be assumed to possess a degree of interest, knowledge and perhaps good will?

And here's another question worth asking:

Where is the reader reading?

On my travels recently, I saw the following in black in white:

Good food is a joy!

I don't know about you, but I couldn't agree more. One slight problem, though: this admirable sentiment was stencilled across the wall of a motorway services cafeteria. And I don't think you have to be an insufferable food-snob to respond as I did: 'Yes, but I'm hungry and can't be bothered to drive any further.'

Poetry in motion

Do you read much poetry at home? Thought not. Very few people do these days.

But, when you're travelling around London, do you ever read those poems on the Underground? Remember:

**What will be read can be dictated
By where your reader is located.**

Again, the relevance to the kind of persuasive writing you're likely to be doing may not be immediately apparent. But it's this: when you sit down to write, you should try as hard as you can to envisage not just what kind of person your reader is, but the circumstances in which she will be reading.

That job application, for example. Do you think an over-worked personnel manager is likely to take it home and sink into her favourite armchair for a leisurely read? Or do you, perhaps, picture her arriving at work on a wet Tuesday morning to find a desk piled high with paper, and 40 emails in her inbox? It'll make a difference to what you write.

Yes, but how does the reader feel?

So far, most of what I've said about understanding your reader has been largely logical. That's to say, I have been trying to persuade you of the importance of using your rational powers to gather relevant information and make reasonable assumptions and intelligent deductions about the kind of person you're addressing.

But logic can only take you so far as a persuasive writer. Readers aren't emotion-free calculating machines. True, they may claim they want nothing but hard facts and compelling arguments, but the truth is that most people, faced with any kind of decision, any choice between different viewpoints or courses of action, listen to their hearts as much as their heads. Of course, the 'heart:head ratio' will vary depending on what's at stake; but it's fair to say that whenever we set out to persuade anyone of anything, we need to consider how we can make our case in a way that appeals at an emotional level, as well as to the intellect.

Take, for example, the current[3] debate about Britain's entry to the Euro. On the face of it, this is an argument that could be resolved on behalf of the British people by an appointed panel of economists and constitutional experts. Would we, as a nation, be better off if we joined? Would exports be healthier? Would interest rates be more stable? Few of us are qualified to answer these questions, so why not leave the decision to those with a really sound grasp of the issues? The answer, of course, is that for the vast majority of us, our own private views on European Monetary Union have very little to do with economics, or

[3]Current at the time of writing, and current I strongly suspect at the time of reading, whenever that may be.

any another 'scientific' consideration. They depend, to a very large extent, on how we feel about Europe and the people who live there; how patriotic we consider ourselves to be (and what we mean by patriotism); and whether 'the pound in our pocket' seems like a reminder of a better time when Britain ruled the waves or a symbol of a stick-in-the-mud country, mired in tradition, left behind by its more go-ahead neighbours.

Me? I love French films; I've just had a wonderful holiday in Spain; and I think the Italians are the most stylish people on earth. I'm convinced that the arguments for joining the Euro are irresistible. See what I mean?

Knowing how your reader is likely to feel about what you have to say is every bit as important as knowing what his job entails or even how knowledgeable he is about the subject.

Logical ways of getting to grips with feeling

In a moment, I'm going to be talking about empathy and intuition. But before we start splashing around in such murky waters, it's worth pausing to note that understanding how your reader is likely to feel is, to quite a large extent, a matter of common sense.

For example, I'm sometimes asked to write various types of employee communication; the means by which a (usually large) company's senior management let the workers know what's going on – why the company has a new logo or is planning to merge with a deadly rival, or whatever. My starting point in such cases is to assume, unless I see powerful evidence to the contrary, that whatever I'm writing will be approached by the workforce with feelings somewhere on the spectrum between healthy scepticism and bitter loathing. If you've ever worked for a large organisation, I'm sure you'll understand why I say that. It's just the natural order of things: except in the rarest cases of supremely enlightened management, the workers despise and, above all, mistrust the bosses. And yet, I've often seen employee communications written in the relentlessly upbeat, onward-and-upward style of a naff corporate press release; full of empty blather about empowering people to do this and raising our sights higher in order to achieve that. I have even – and I swear I'm not making this up – recently seen an all-staff memo from the senior partner of a large law firm announcing 50 imminent redundancies, but attempting to cast this in a positive light as part of the firm's clearly defined strategy of ever greater client-focus. ('Great! My being fired will ensure my former clients get a better service!') So, up to a point, logical left-brain thinking can help us get to grips with how our reader may feel about whatever we have to say. But what if we want to go beyond that point?

Tuning in to the reader's emotional wavelength

Good persuasive writers do this instinctively. They find out what they can about their reader; they make reasonable assumptions and intelligent deductions about why, when and where she'll be reading; they think logically about how she is likely to feel towards what they have to say. And then they do something much less easily explained: they make an imaginative leap that enables them to 'tune in' to the emotion – or set of emotions – that is most likely to have a bearing on the success or failure of a particular piece of communication. Let me give you an example of what I mean.

A while ago, I saw an advertisement for an American airline which was introducing seats with extra leg room in economy class. With this brief, the headline of the ad might well have read:

Stretch your legs. Without over-extending your budget.

Or even:

Beat Deep Vein Thrombosis. At prices that won't give you a heart attack.

But, in fact, what the copywriter had written was:

News just in. Not all tall people are rich.

As quite a tall person who's far from rich, this struck a resounding chord with me. Because, as anyone who has ever walked through business class on the way back to the cramped, knees-under-chin squalor of economy will know, air travel is all about class warfare. We, the proletariat, hate those smug bastards at the front of the plane, and they look down on us. And, by understanding this basic emotional truth, this ad made a strong and immediate connection with me.

This tuning in thing: how's it done?

I don't know. I'm pretty sure that empathy – because that is what we're talking about here – is something that good persuasive writers, and indeed all good communicators, are born with. As I suggested above, they don't have to make a conscious effort to do this. The ability to put themselves in another person's place – to see through that person's eyes – comes naturally to them. (Conversely, I'm convinced that some people are born without it. And, in most cases, they seem perversely proud of the fact, blundering around, trampling on people's feelings, then congratulating themselves on 'telling it like it is' or 'calling a spade a spade'.)

Can empathy be learned? Well, up to about GCSE level, perhaps. After all, just as there are allegedly only seven basic plotlines, there are relatively few basic human emotions. So, in theory, there's no reason why a con-scientious student shouldn't acquire a sound working knowledge of what they are and how to recognise them. I used to work for a small communications consultancy run, rather bizarrely, by a trained zoologist. He claimed that he could apply scientific methodology to identify what he called 'primal drives' – i.e. the emotions that determine buying decisions in any market. These might be: the urge to protect one's young; the desire for supremacy over a rival; a wish to stand out from the crowd; and so on. Once identified, the relevant primal drive could, according to my client, be triggered by ingeniously designed communications – resulting, hey presto, in the recipient rushing out, blank-eyed zombie-style, to buy a new car, open a savings account, order a new prosthetic limb, or whatever.

Despite my facetious[4] tone, I think my client did have a point: I agree that, in any situation where one person wants to win over another to his point of view, there will usually be one predominant emotion that will determine the outcome. But I'm always suspicious of any attempt to reduce the art of persuasive communication to a science. The best persuasive writers don't simply analyse the available data in order to arrive at a logical conclusion about which emotion will enable them to make a connection with their readers; they use that inborn empathy to feel their way into the mind of their imagined reader. They actually feel what the reader is feeling. It's an emotional and intuitive process, not a detached and objective one. And, as a result, it can provide the writer with a much deeper level of insight into what's going on inside the reader's head. The airline ad mentioned earlier, for example, could never have been written without this kind of empathy; scientific analysis alone would never have suggested the 'class war' approach to this particular piece of communication.

[4]Apparently, there are five words in the English language in which the five vowels appear once each in alphabetical order. Apart from this one, I've got 'abstemious'. Any ideas about the other three?

I don't want to labour this, because I'm conscious how pretentious it could sound. Persuasive writers aren't Artists. But there *is* an art to persuasive writing; and the very best exponents of it aren't those who know the most long words or the difference between a semi-colon and a comma; but those who can blend rigorous logic with real empathy to present their case in a way that doesn't just make perfect sense, but also feels exactly right.

So, to recap ...

When we write persuasively, it's essential to start with the clearest possible picture of our reader, and to keep that picture firmly in mind as we write.

When we know the individual concerned, this is easy. But when we're talking to a stranger – or an audience made up of strangers – we need to make a much more conscious effort to arrive at a sense of who our reader is, and how we can make whatever we have to say engaging and persuasive to her.

This process requires both logical, analytic thinking and a degree of intuition and empathy. The former will enable us to gather relevant information, make decisions about what our persuasive priorities are, and make reasonable assumptions and deductions about our reader based on what we know. The latter will allow us to tune into the reader's emotional wavelength, and anticipate the gut level responses that, in many cases, will decide the outcome of an attempt at persuasive communication.

School report-speak: a language that nobody talks

Remember Lily from chapter one? Well, I've asked her permission, and she says it's OK for me to reproduce part of her most recent school report. Here it is:

Mathematics – Lily can identify and obtain necessary information, make mathematical statements and explain her reasoning. She has a sound knowledge of the four rules. She is able to work out problems in her head. She can draw on her experience to make sensible estimates in measurement. She collects and records data, interprets graphs and draws conclusions based on findings. She understands and uses vocabulary associated with probability.

Er, right. So should I be impressed that she has 'a sound knowledge of the four rules' – or is this standard stuff for a child of her age? (And what the hell are the four rules, anyway?) Is drawing on her experience to 'make sensible estimates in measurement' a good thing, or should she be using a ruler? And does the fact that she 'understands and uses vocabulary associated with probability' make her a junior Einstein?

It sounds like it, but I have no way of knowing. In fact, there's absolutely nothing here that tells me anything which, as Lily's father, I might want to know about her performance in maths – like how she's been getting on, or whether she's any good at the subject.

Of course, it's not the individual teacher's fault. Primary school reports these days are written not to inform parents, but to satisfy government-imposed National Curriculum criteria. No doubt an OFSTED inspector would have found my daughter's report highly illuminating. But, addressed to me, it might as well have read:

$$dX(t) = a(t,X[t])dt + \sigma(t,X[t])dB(t)$$

In short, this process is – to some extent, at least – an imaginative or creative one. Perhaps we might even say that, a bit like the way a novelist invents a protagonist, good persuasive writers conjure up in their mind's eye a character called The Reader, with the aim of enabling themselves to write with all the advantages of addressing somebody they know.

Yes, but surely that's total rubbish?

No, I don't think it is. I only said it was a bit like what a novelist does. And, if you check the paragraph above, I didn't claim that good persuasive writers can always really 'know' the reader they are addressing; just that they aim to, as far as possible.

In my experience, I have to say, that often isn't very far at all. Most of the things I write professionally are aimed at target audiences made up of hundreds, thousands or even millions of individuals. Try as I may, distilling this mass of humanity into a single, fully imagined Composite Reader, whose interests, attitudes and feelings are an open book to me, whose lifestyle and tastes I understand, whose TV viewing habits I am familiar with, whose every whim I can anticipate ... well, sadly, most of the time, it just ain't going to happen.

Usually, when I write, the reader I'm addressing is actually a fairly shadowy figure; less a person than a presence. It may sound like a dodgy séance, but what I have is a strong sense that there is 'somebody there'. Usually a faceless, nameless, even genderless somebody, defined by only a handful of characteristics.

What are these characteristics? Some of the most important are the 'constants' that I mentioned at the beginning of this chapter: you can never remind yourself too often, for example, that your reader is not an idiot. But, depending on the project, there will always be something else which I know about the reader that will be of the greatest importance to me in making a connection with her. Sometimes, this will be factual in nature; hard information that helps me understand why, when or where the reader will be reading. But, nearly always, the key is the emotional stuff, and there are two reasons for this.

The first is the obvious one: feelings weigh more than rational thought. Since most people make most decisions more on the basis of gut instinct than logical analysis, it follows that tuning into the reader's emotional wavelength gives the persuasive writer the best chance of success.

But the second reason is no less important: feelings unite people. Take 10,000 people and ask them what they think should be done about global warming, or which member of Girls Aloud has the best chance of a decent solo career, and you'll get dozens of different answers. (Well, up to five, anyway, in the case of Girls Aloud.) Show them a picture of a cute kitten, and at least 9995 of them will go, 'Aaaah!' Our emotional responses define our common humanity. And, this being the case, they represent the persuasive writer's best hope of finding common ground on which to meet the reader. And the larger and more diverse the target audience for a piece of writing, the more true this becomes. When a writer addresses a truly mass audience – pensioners, police officers, partners in City law firms, pedicurists, paediatricians, podiatrists, publicans, production managers, pimps, to mention just the Ps – the only way of making a connection will be by finding a common emotional thread.

Perhaps this doesn't sound very much. Perhaps you're thinking that, after wittering on about understanding your reader for page after page, I've reached the conclusion that actually, in many cases, it's almost impossible to arrive at anything more than a very hazy picture of this elusive individual.

But, however blurred around the edges that picture may be, it's all you've got to work with, as a persuasive writer. You may know very little about the kind of person your reader is; about why, when and where she'll be reading; and about how much she knows, how interested she is and what her feelings are likely to be. But the little you do know will, very largely, determine how successful you will be in winning her over to your point of view.

'So how do you picture me, your reader?'

I was afraid you might ask me that. Because the truth is, the image I have in my mind's eye of you – the reader of this book – is much less distinct than I would like it to be. I would love to be able to leave you reeling with astonishment at the accuracy of my pen portrait of you ('My god, how could he possibly know that I'm a 37-year-old mother of two with blonde highlights, a degree from Newcastle University, a Vauxhall Corsa and a few painful unresolved issues around my relationship with my mother?') Sadly, though, that won't be possible. But I will tell you what I do know about you. Or perhaps I should say what I think and feel I know.

As far as biographical details are concerned, almost nothing. You could be male or female, and any age from maybe 18 (Hi, Harry!) to 75 (Hello, Mum!). It's possible that you work in the communications business, or any other business where communications are important (er, which actually means every business); but, since the whole point of this book is to demonstrate that the principles which apply to professionally produced communications can be also be applied to virtually any kind of non-creative writing, I certainly don't see you as someone who wants to make a living as a persuasive writer. (Although if you are, I hope you'll find this book helpful.)

Not much to go on, then, so far. But, as I've said at some length, factual information about the reader is usually only of limited value to a persuasive writer. So let's turn instead to my assumptions, deductions, wild guesses and weird spooky feelings about you.

Why are you reading? I think you probably picked up this book because you thought it might be useful to you. It's quite likely that somebody recommended it to you. If you thought it might be useful, that probably means – though not necessarily – that you felt it might help you in your working life; which, in turn suggests, that you had at least some inkling of how 'persuasive writing' could be relevant to you.

My guess, though, is that I may have almost lost you early on. Because, having picked up the book expecting to learn something useful, you must have realised very quickly that this isn't by any stretch of the imagination a 'how to do it' manual. But, being of enquiring mind, you gave me the benefit of the doubt; and after perhaps half a dozen pages, I think you may have begun to find it a bit thought-provoking, and quite fun to read, too. If you remember the Useful/Interesting/Enjoyable equation, I suspect that as U diminished, both I and E increased proportionately, giving the result: worth continuing to read.

When are you reading? My only assumption here is that you are at a fairly early stage in the 'buying process'. That's to say, I see you as someone with an intelligent layperson's interest in the subject matter of this book, rather than an in-depth professional or academic knowledge.

What about the emotions at work in the relationship that I am trying to form with you? Well, I've hinted at one already. I think that, by picking up this book in the first place, you demonstrated quite a powerful urge for self-improvement. Most people read Catherine Cookson or Harry Potter (or nothing at all). You believe – and please don't be embarrassed by this – that you could be better than you are, and you're prepared to put time and effort into achieving that.

There's something else, too. You believe in the power of words. You must, or you wouldn't be reading this. You have a strong sense that the ability to express yourself better, to present your point of view more powerfully, to use words to make closer connections with other people, could be of the greatest value to you.

And that, actually, is all I really need to know about you.

Chapter 4
Writing for results

Why being very, very clear about what you're trying to achieve is a good idea, and what can go wrong if you aren't; the difference between the result you want and the response that will make it more likely; why readers need to be rewarded; and the importance for persuasive writers of remembering that it's a competitive world out there.

A couple of years ago, I became involved in a dispute with a builder. As you do. I felt that – having over-run the original schedule by about nine months and over-spent the agreed budget by roughly 40% – he was being a little unreasonable in sending me yet another enormous invoice. He felt that I was a slippery, cheating, ungrateful bastard.

We both did a bit of shouting on the phone, and then we started writing letters. At first, I tried – honestly – to be non-confrontational; to explain, clearly and coolly, why I was fully entitled to withhold payment, and to make him see the error of his ways.

It didn't work. My opponent persisted in his stubborn belief that I should sell my children into slavery in order to pay his final, outrageous invoice. And, rather to my surprise, he wrote quite good, very long letters in support of his case – somewhat in the style of a self-important provincial solicitor ('I am therefore obliged to restate the position as it pertains to the monies withheld ...).

Our correspondence continued for a while, punctuated by a few more angry phone calls. And then two things occurred to me.

First, I realised that, while I was upset and anxious about the dispute, my opponent was enjoying it. Writing long, pompous letters in self-justifying legal-speak was clearly a welcome distraction from the tedious and time-consuming business of actually building things for people.

Second, and much worse, I realised that I'd completely lost sight of my objective. By this time, I had probably written half a dozen letters. I had also lost quite a bit of sleep. But, actually, from the outset, there had only ever been two options: I could pay him the ludicrous sum he was demanding, or see him in court.

Everything else was wasted words.

For a persuasive writer, it's the most basic mistake in the book: sitting down to write without a really clear picture of the intended result. But if this gnarled professional can make such a schoolboy error, so can just about any-one. And believe me, it happens all the time. Vast swathes of supposedly persuasive writing fail to persuade anybody of anything because the writer has neglected to answer (or perhaps even ask) the question:

What, specifically, am I trying to achieve here?

Actually, I think this fundamental foul-up can be seen to take at least four slightly different forms:

- Not knowing what the intended result is, in the first place
- Losing sight of the intended result, somewhere along the way
- Not being single-minded enough about the intended result
- Not being realistic about the intended result

Let's look, briefly, at each of these ...

Not knowing what the intended result is, in the first place

This is most likely to happen when a persuasive writer doesn't realise that he is a persuasive writer. That's to say, it's a simple failure to recognise that a piece of writing has the potential to influence its reader.

How can this come about? It can be an innocent mistake; a misguided belief that the purpose of a particular piece of writing is solely 'informative'. I remember on more than one occasion being asked by clients to write ads that would 'just announce' the opening of a new store, say, or

And the award for most effective use of language in a shop doorway goes to ...

It occurred to me today when I went to buy the bread that, of all the people I know who use language to give themselves an advantage over the competition, few do it more effectively than the young guy who begs outside the baker's shop.

Perhaps, hearing that, you imagine him handing out a leaflet, explaining the sad circumstances that have led to a life on the streets. Or, at least, wearing a sign around his neck, saying 'homeless and hungry please help'.

But, actually, the way he uses words is much simpler than that. He just says, 'How are you today?' And unless you're a truly horrible person, you reply, 'Fine, how about you?' And suddenly, you're having a conversation – and realising that this young man with his nice smile, and watery blue eyes, and catastrophic teeth, is not some faceless member of a feckless underclass, but somebody's barely post-teenage son, whose life has gone badly wrong – temporarily, perhaps – and who needs 50p much more than you do.

In other words, he uses language in a way that engages his target audience, and establishes a relationship. Note, in particular, that 'today' on the end of his question. 'How are you?' is bland, a generic greeting, easy to brush off; 'How are you today?' is sharper, particular to the moment, much harder to sidestep. It implies that a relationship already exists between you.

And it does. Over the last year or so, I must have given him twice as much I've given to all the other beggars on Gloucester Road put together.

even the launch of a new product. Not possible. Advertising is, by definition, persuasive communication; it's always selling something – even when its immediate purpose isn't to talk the customer into making a purchase. An ad that doesn't persuade is like a fish that doesn't swim: dead in the water.

But, more often, when writing shows no sign of having any clearly defined objective, it's because the writer is so wrapped up in his own agenda – what his interests are, how he sees the world, how committed he is to this or dedicated to that – that he simply isn't relating to his reader at all. And if you're writing without a powerful sense of an ever-present reader, why would you concern yourself with the result you are trying to achieve? The only result that you're interested in is a world that's a little more up to date with what's going on in your life.

Losing sight of the intended result

My building dispute illustrates this pretty well. I'm fairly sure I knew what my goal was when the correspondence started, but by the third or fourth letter I was writing for no other reason than to vent some of the pent-up rage I was feeling – oh yes, and to tear to shreds the manifestly false logic of the argument put forward by my adversary in paragraph three of his most recent communication …

Of course, it's easy to forget what you're fighting for in the heat of battle. But it isn't only when the red mist descends that writers make this mistake. In professional persuasive writing, it often happens when the client has something he is particularly proud of – a new manu-facturing process, an award for innovation in the plastics industry, a new bottling plant just outside Kettering, or whatever. True, these things may be relevant to the reader, in which case including them could well help to bring about the desired result. But often, the writer duti-fully gives them a mention because – well, because the client's expecting to see them, and he's paying, after all. Never mind that every irrelevant word makes the desired result less likely.

When we write on our own account, there's no actual flesh and blood client to blame. But perhaps we all have an 'inner client'; a little voice inside our heads, promp-ting us to say more than we need to achieve the result we want; to tell our reader what we want them to know rather than what they might be interested to hear.

Not being single-minded enough about the intended result

In the previous chapter, I talked about the need to be ruthless in defining your target audience; the importance of zeroing in on the individual (or type of individual) reader you most want to persuade. Exactly the same applies to results. The more focused you can be about what your objective is, the greater your chance of success.

In fact, it's fair to say that the best persuasive communication is always single-minded. It sets itself one specific, clearly defined goal – and it doesn't let anything get in the way of achieving this.

Don't misunderstand me; it's perfectly possible for a good piece of persuasive writing to achieve more than one objective. But the important thing is that the writer must always be clear about the main aim, and treat everything else as a lower priority.

Not being realistic about the intended result

A couple of years ago, I was asked to work on a new advertising campaign for a client in the water cooler business. (Warning: some product categories have been changed to protect the feelings of incredibly stupid clients.) The objective of the advertising was ambitious: the client wanted nothing less than to 'change the way that people think about water coolers'.

Advertising can, actually, achieve such aims. Sometimes. When it's brilliantly conceived, meticulously executed and perfectly timed to connect with a receptiveness to change out there in the world at large ... oh yes, and when the client is prepared to spend a lot of money. This one wasn't. He wanted us to change the way the British public perceived not just his product but the entire category of product to which it belonged, in one small black and white advertisement, measuring roughly 10 centimetres by 15.

It's an extreme example, but the same thing happens all the time: clients and agencies setting themselves absurd, unfeasible goals. In a way, it's understandable. Clients quite naturally want the money they spend on advertising to produce dramatic results; they want sales to quadruple overnight, and to keep on doing so night after night, until each of their competitors in turn is forced into bankruptcy, and total market domination is theirs. Agencies, almost as understandably – though less forgivably – are reluctant to admit that the ads they produce may fall short of delivering such a desirable outcome. So the two sides conspire to produce advertising which aims ludicrously high, and falls catastrophically (and inevitably) short.

Be realistic when you decide what result you want your writing to achieve. Ask yourself, given what I know about my reader, and the strength of the arguments available to me, and my skill as a writer, how likely is it that I can accomplish this objective? Better still, put yourself in your reader's shoes. Now, what are the chances that you could be persuaded?

Hmm. In that case, you need to rethink the result you're after.

If you don't want to know the results, look away now

Let's look at a few examples of some things that you might want to write, and the kind of results you might reasonably set out to achieve:

- Job application. Intended result: secure an interview. (NB Not secure the job – a small, but significant distinction.)
- Email advising a client of potential risks inherent in a proposed course of action. Intended result: cover your arse.
- Flyer for school summer fair. Intended result: 10% more attendees than last year.
- Letter to former boss asking for a reference. Intended result: glowing reference from former boss.
- Poster asking for information on missing cat. Intended result: information leading to return of missing cat.
- Angry letter to bank having just been refused new, much increased overdraft facility. Intended result: to have your say, get it off your chest, let off steam. (NB This is a perfectly reasonable objective, provided you are clear that this is what you want to achieve.)

What Mrs Powell taught me about good writing

When I was a young, tender, immature, callow, pre-pubescent lad of 11, I went to secondary school, where I was taught English by an elderly, venerable, crabby lady called Mrs Powell.

Mrs Powell was very keen on adjectives. Her decided, firm, pronounced view was that good, talented, accomplished writers should use a lot of them. And she always gave high, elevated, top marks to anyone who did.

I quickly grasped this. So every time I wrote a composition for her I made sure it was stuffed with a plentiful, huge, abundant number of adjectives – not all of them apt, bouncy or appropriate. As a result, I soon became Mrs Powell's favourite, preferred, pre-eminent pupil – or teacher's pet, as we used to say in those far-off days.

The moral of the story is not, of course, that good writers should use a lot of adjectives. It's the point that (I know) I risk boring you to death with: that, in order to get the result you want, you need to understand your reader.

If these examples seem trite to you, I'm unabashed. Because it really doesn't matter in the slightest what the result you decide to aim for may be; only that you're very clear about what is; that you never lose sight of it; that you don't allow secondary objectives to cloud the issue; and that it's realistically achievable.

Another reason why knowing the result you want is a good idea

In a moment, I'm going to say quite a bit more about how knowing the result you want affects what you write. But first, let's pause to acknowledge another seemingly obvious but often ignored reason why a clearly defined objective is of value:

> Because if you don't know what you are trying to achieve in a piece of writing, it's impossible to judge how far you have succeeded.

Did you get an interview for that job? How many tickets were sold for the summer fair? Was there any milk on the doorstep next morning? The more specific and measurable the result, the easier it is to evaluate your performance as a persuasive writer.

The fourth 'R' of good persuasive writing?

I wonder if, over the last few pages, you may have noticed an apparent flaw in my argument? If so, I think I know what it might be. I suspect the insistent little voice inside your head that I was talking about earlier may well have been muttering something like, 'OK, I can see why not being clear about the result you want from a piece of writing is a bad idea. But I don't really see why the reverse is true; how knowing what result you want actually helps you achieve it. Wanting something isn't the same as getting it. It's a bit like saying just because I know that I want Crystal Palace to beat Arsenal on Saturday, that means they will.'

If that thought, or anything like it, has crossed your mind, I admit you have a point. Because there is, if not a flaw, then at least a gap in the argument I've presented so far; something else that good persuasive writers have to do between deciding on the result they want and achieving it.

Response: the moment when the result you want becomes a possibility

The result of a piece of persuasive writing is what happens next; how the reader thinks, feels or behaves after she has finished reading (whether immediately afterwards, a short while later, or after an interval of many years). The response, on the other hand, is what goes on inside the reader's head while she is actually reading.

This is a crucial distinction. Why? Because, as we've acknowledged, the result is clearly something that no writer, however persuasive, can have any control over. Once the reader has finished reading, it's out of the writer's hands: whether the reader goes out and buys Brand X, votes for the Monster Raving Loony Party, or makes a donation to the Sunny Meadows Home for Retired Police Horses is entirely up to her.

But while the reader is actually reading, it's a different matter: a good writer can hope to evoke a specific response – which may make the intended result more likely.

Like so much else in this book, the basic principle of what I'm saying here is incredibly simple. Person reads advert. Thinks: 'Hmm, this Brand X sounds worth a try.' (Response.) Goes to shop, buys large quantity of Brand X. (Result.)

But, in practice, it's quite a lot more complicated than that for two main reasons.

What response is most likely to lead to the intended result?

Sadly, most people are rather more complex psychologically than my enthusiastic Brand X convert above. And very rarely as persuasive writers can we hope to identify a response that will lead directly and infallibly to the result we want.

To illustrate what I mean, let's look briefly at another of the examples I mentioned above.

It's local election time. You're a passionate supporter of the Monster Raving Loony Party, living in a ward held by Labour with a majority of 5,000. You're writing a flyer. You know the result you want: one more vote than Labour. But what is the response which is most likely to enable you to achieve your aim? What is the specific feeling or thought process which, if you can succeed in triggering it, will get local voters off their backsides and down to the polling station, ready to put their mark next to your candidate's name?

Tricky. It might be: 'These Monster Raving Loonies sound fantastic – I agree with everything they say, I'll definitely vote for them.'

Or: 'As far as I'm concerned, education is the big issue locally – and it sounds as if the MRL party are closest to my views. I think I'll vote for them.'

Or: 'God, I'd like to poke Tony Blair (or Harriet Harman, or Jade from *Big Brother*, or whoever is Labour leader by the time you read this) in the eye with a sharp stick. But, failing that, a vote for the MRL party would teach him a lesson – even if it's only a local election.'

Of course, there isn't a single correct answer to this hypothetical problem. When we write persuasively, there may be several – or even many – possible responses which may help us achieve the result we want. And it's up to us to decide which is the best bet.

So what do you write to trigger the desired response?

And so, at last, we come to the place where any piece of persuasive writing succeeds or fails. Not the printed page or the PC screen, but the inside of the reader's head. Because, as a persuasive writer, what you write really doesn't matter at all; only how your reader responds.

To demonstrate what I mean by that, I thought we might turn our attention to the personal columns. You know the kind of thing:

Guy, 37, Mayfair apartment, GSOH, wltm ...

Presumably, our friend in search of love here is indeed a 'guy'. (Why would he lie about that?) He might perhaps be knocking a year or two off his real age; and, as for the flat, it sounds frankly a bit implausible. But, since such things can be proved one way or another, and only a cretin would risk being caught out in a bare-faced lie, let's give him the benefit of the doubt. What are we supposed to make, though, of that old lonely hearts column stand-by, 'GSOH'?

Yes, of course, it stands for good sense of humour. But what does Would-be Lover Boy intend to communicate by that? A few possibilities might include:

• 'I was recently appointed Life President of the Jim Davidson Fan Club.'

- 'I'm very proud of my collection of amusing bow ties.'
- 'I can quote whole episodes of Monty Python off–by-heart. Shall I?'
- 'I set fire to my best mate's beard last night. Laugh? I nearly wet myself.'

The fact that one person has a good sense of humour can no more be communicated to another by means of a four letter abbreviation than a C major chord can be carved in stone or the smell of a freshly bathed baby captured in computer code. All our Lonely Heart has succeeded in communicating is that he thinks he has a good sense of humour; not the same thing at all.

The problem, of course, lies with that unco-operative individual I talked about in the last chapter, the Reader Who Always Reads Between The Lines. When the RWARBTL reads that her prospective lover possesses a 'GSOH', her response isn't 'Ooh, lovely, a man who can make me laugh'; it's 'I'll be the judge of that, buster.'

So how might a Lonely Hearts advertiser successfully communicate a good sense of humour? There's only one way: by writing something that demonstrates it. Like this, for example, which recently appeared in the *London Review of Books*:

People who use museum postcards instead of letter-paper; people who own garden composters; mechanics called Andy who get stroppy over the phone if you call during their lunch hour, fully expecting you to know that they take lunch between ten and 11 in the morning; people who shoehorn obscure French novelists into any conversation; people who take over-sized stroller push-chairs on the Northern Line at rush-hour and get shirty when other passengers refuse to dislocate their limbs and fold themselves up in the corner to make room; news-paper supplement journalists who begin every article like they're writing a novel in the hope that a literary agent will snap them up; literary agents who snap up newspaper supplement journalists believing that their opening para-graphs would make an excellent start to a novel; the girl at Superdrug who never tells me how much my items come to but expects me to succumb to the power of her mind and make me look at the little screen on her till instead; postmen who make a concerted effort to bend packages with 'do not bend' clearly stamped across the front; Bob Wilson; thirtysomethings who listen to Radio-head, believing that Thom Yorke's depressing introspection has revolutionised the British music scene and made rock energetic once again without realising that Dire Straits fans were saying exactly the same thing about them in the early Eighties; people who buy organic mushrooms; people who subscribe to magazines and get excited every time a new one lands on the doormat; people who have doormats; people who applaud the linesman's offside flag; people with more than one cat; people who have bought radiator covers; people who frame museum postcards sent by people who use them instead of letter-paper; people who own a copy of Michael Palin's 'Pole to Pole' on DVD. Everybody else write to man, 37. Box No 257.

> 'Writing something doesn't mean you have communicated it; not writing it doesn't mean you haven't.'
>
> Jeremy Bullmore

Well, it makes me laugh. But, of course, this is a high risk strategy, because humour is notoriously subjective. That's what good persuasive writers do, though: they write what they believe will elicit the desired response (in this case, a laugh or at least a smile) from the reader, thus increasing the chances of achieving the result they want (in this case, a reply to Box 257).

This is such an important point that I'm going to risk saying it again in an only very slightly different way:

> Good persuasive writers don't tell their readers what to think or feel; they say something that makes their readers feel or think it for themselves.

And when we write persuasively, every word we use has the potential to trigger a response – positive or negative – in our reader. Yes, all of them. Even the most apparently neutral word or phrase often comes with baggage. Consider, for example, the fact that our man with the alleged GSOH chose to describe himself as a 'guy'. Are you the kind of gal who wltm a guy? Or would you, perhaps, prefer a chap, a bloke, a fella, a dude, a geezer or even a man?

And it's even worse than that, because it's not just all the words we use that can make the response – and therefore the result – we want more, or less likely. So can the words we don't use.

Reward: quite possibly the fifth R of good persuasive writing

Do you remember that in the previous chapter, I talked about the way in which readers continually calculate whether what they stand to gain from a piece of writing will compensate for the time it will cost them to read it? Good, because I want to develop this idea of rewarding the reader a little further.

Probably the most obvious sense in which a reader gets a return on her investment of time is if she takes something of value away from a piece of writing – information that will help her in her work; an inspiring idea; a foolproof recipe for hollandaise sauce, or whatever. But there's also a much more immediate way that good persuasive writing can reward the reader. Here's an example of how not to do it.

Perhaps you recall (though, on balance, you probably don't) a recent advertisement for a well-known fast food chain that showed an expensive looking photograph of a box of eggs, conspicuously marked 'free range', and over this a headline reading:

Which came first, the chicken or the egg? We think it's the chicken.

Putting aside the issue of whether a famously litigious retailer of sugar-laden, fat-drenched, heart attack-inducing, tastebud-bypassing pap should really be wasting millions of its shareholders' money attempting to convince us of its concern for animal welfare, this ad fails disastrously as a piece of persuasive communication. Why? Because it leaves the reader nothing whatsoever to do. It asks a familiar question; and then, goofily, it answers it.

The photograph tells us the eggs are free range. We all know the old conundrum about 'which came first … ' So all the headline needed to say was something like:

For us, the chicken always comes first.

Then we, as readers, would have supplied the rest. And, in doing so – in decoding the reference, and 'completing' the communication – we would have experienced a very, very small frisson of pleasure. ('Ah yes, I get it – which came first, the chicken or the egg?')

Good persuasive writers make the reader a collaborator

Actually, all written communication is collaborative, when you think about it. I'm sitting here making marks appear on my screen, you're sitting there deciphering them on the page, and supplying their meaning. I couldn't do it without you. And the same would apply whatever I might be writing, from a sonnet to a software user's manual.

But what I'm talking about here is the need for persuasive writers to make the reader a *willing* collaborator, by writing in such a way that she finds it enjoyable or satisfying to participate in an intimate act; communication between two people.

What this means, perhaps surprisingly, is that quite often the best persuasive writing is not – as it's commonly supposed to be – the most straightforward, direct and unambiguous. Because, as we've just seen, when we spell things out, we risk depriving our reader of any possible pleasure or reward. Rather than a willing participant, she becomes a hapless bystander; someone who just happens to be standing in the path of an unstoppable torrent of words unleashed by us.

I'll be talking quite a bit in the next section about some of the ways in which persuasive writers can make the reader into a willing collaborator. So for now, perhaps it's enough to establish a general principle – which is that when we write persuasively we need to deliberately leave 'space' in our work to allow the RWARBTL (you remember, the Reader Who Always Reads Between The Lines) to roam freely. Because, as a willing collaborator, there's a far better chance that she will respond in the way we want – which, in turn, will make the result we're aiming for more likely.

Catch!

As so often, the conventional wisdom is hopelessly wrong: the best writing isn't always direct, straight-forward, to the point.

In many cases, writing works better when its true meaning is implied rather than explicitly stated; when it hints and suggests rather than hammering home its point. Of course, when we write 'indirectly', it's possible that the reader won't understand what we're saying. But it's very often a risk worth taking.

To explain why, let's borrow my friend David Stuart's famous Ball Throwing Analogy. If you and I stand a metre apart and I throw a ball to you very gently, you will almost certainly catch it. If, on the other hand, you stand 30 metres away, and I chuck the ball as high in the air as I can, catching it will be a lot harder. But which catch will be a more rewarding experience? Which will you be more likely to remember?

Writing that expresses meaning 'indirectly' is like the ball thrown high into the air. There's a risk you may drop it. But if you make ground to your left, throw yourself full length and cling on by your fingertips, you'll get a lot more out of the experience.

Good writing is about judging how difficult to make the catch.

Content: you guessed, it's all about your reader

As you may have noticed, so far I've said a lot more about how to write than about what to write. For example, a few pages back, I gave our friend with the aching void in his love life a kicking not for claiming to have a good sense of humour, but for the way in which he attempted to communicate it.

But if he had possessed the skills to capture in words his encyclopaedic knowledge of Benny Hill's work or his love of malicious practical jokes, or whatever it was he meant by GSOH, would that have been the right thing to focus on in his advertisement? Well, possibly. But only if his main aim in advertising was to get replies from potential partners who shared his particular kind of SOH.

Sorry, once again, if that sounds gob-smackingly obvious. But bad writers get this wrong all the time. They sit down to write thinking, 'What do I want to tell my reader?' Good ones think, 'What do I have to say which will help to get the result I want?' Or perhaps, rather more long-windedly, 'What do I have to say which, bearing in mind what I know about my reader, will trigger the response that's most likely to lead to the result I want?'

In short, what a persuasive writer writes is dictated by the reader and the result, no less than how a persuasive writer writes.

If it doesn't make the result you want more likely, leave it out

Does this sound cynical? I hope not. Because I'm absolutely not advocating lying, distorting the facts or in any way being economical with the truth. On the contrary, I'm talking about the vital importance for persuasive writers of being brutally honest with themselves; of looking at the story they have to tell and asking themselves what they can (truthfully) say that their reader might conceivably find interesting, useful or enjoyable. And then, discarding absolutely everything else.

I don't care if you have a great sense of humour, a degree in History of Art, in-depth knowledge of Neuro Linguistic Programming, over 20 years' experience in fund management, a Mark 4 Cortina in mint condition or a revolutionary new low temperature smelting technique; unless it makes the result you want more likely, out it goes.

So what should you include, in the way of content, next time you sit down to write persuasively? Hard for me to answer, since I don't know whether you're planning a passionate polemic in support of animal rights or a poster for a car boot sale. But I can give you one piece of positive advice about how to arrive at what you should be saying …

Remember that all persuasive writing is competitive

In my line of work, that goes without saying. All commercial organisations have competitors, so when I write about their products or services, it's safe to assume that their customers will want to know what makes them different from/better than those of their competitors. That, in essence, is what advertising does. Sometimes, it does this job in a very direct, gloves-off kind of way, drawing direct comparisons ('Why buy crummy old Brand X, with its obsolete technology, when you can have our new whizzy state-of-the-art model for the same price?'). But even when the advertiser doesn't resort to 'knocking copy' – and most don't, for fear of getting into a fight they might lose – the basic aim is the same: to present a case that gives the potential customer a reason for choosing the product or service in question, in preference to others of a similar kind.

And I can't think of any kind of true persuasive writing where the same principle doesn't apply. Of course, depending on what you're writing, you may not have competitors in the same sense as a company advertising its new range of organic ready meals, or its online garden design business. But whatever you're selling – your religious beliefs, an idea for restructuring your company's salesforce, that old fridge-freezer cluttering up the cellar – your reader always has other options.

So, before you write, you need to be very clear about what, from your reader's point of view, your competitive advantage actually is.

What if there's no competitive advantage?

I said a moment ago that, in the world of professional persuasive communication, the need for a clear competitive advantage is self-evident. But actually, that isn't quite true. You'd be amazed how often I've attended briefing sessions where none of the highly paid advertising and marketing people present has been able to give me one really good reason why our target audience should choose the product or service in question. 'To be honest,' they confide, looking around to make sure they won't be overheard, 'there really isn't anything that special or different about it.'

Perhaps I'm supposed to be won over by such refreshing candour; but I'm not. Because I believe that unless you can make a case for whatever you're selling that sets it apart from its competitors, then you should save your breath.

The problem, of course, is that in most fields real, sharply defined points of difference between one product and another are in short supply. One washing powder is pretty much like another. And these days, when good ideas are quickly imitated, the same increasingly applies to computers, prepared salads and off-set mortgages.

So what's to be done when your 'product' doesn't have an obvious edge over its rivals?

In search of the USP

Way back in advertising history, one of the big ad American agencies tackled this problem by inventing something called the Unique Selling Proposition (or USP). As the name suggests, the idea was to formulate an offer or promise to the potential customer that no competitor could duplicate. And they rigorously applied this formula for effective advertising to every product they advertised. No ad could ever be produced unless it contained a USP.

This resulted in some fairly bizarre claims. For example, I fondly remember (though you're probably too young) the chocolate bar that promised us 'a hazelnut in every bite'. Was this claim true? Did exhaustive testing take place in order to substantiate it? And, if so, how many bites, of what size, did the testers take before they were satisfied that this particular USP stood up?

No matter. In that earlier, more innocent age, it was enough, apparently, for advertisers to look closely at their product and find something – anything – that could be seen to set it apart. How much times have changed can be seen from a more recent confectionery commercial which ended, you may remember, with Vic Reeves informing us that the chocolate bar in question was 'flat, with a slightly rippled underside' – a post-modern USP if ever there was one.

No gobbledegook? No thanks!

Not sure whether that uncomfortable feeling is my heart sinking or my hackles rising. But I do know who's to blame. It's yet another bank expensively relaunching itself on a 'no gobbledegook' platform. There it is in my paper this morning, taking two full pages to inform me that it has three mortgage types which can be adapted to my situation – and which they will be happy to explain 'in language that actually makes sense'.

Is there anything special or different about their mortgages? No, or they would have told me. All they have to offer is a promise that they won't use any long, confusing words that might make my head spin.

How breathtakingly patronising is that? A bank that communicated clearly and comprehensibly with its customers, in a way that treated them like intelligent adults, would have a genuine point of difference. Not so a bank that spends millions noisily congratulating itself on its alleged communication skills.

'You must be the change you want to see in the world', said Gandhi. For our purposes, that should read: you must be the change you want to make in people's minds.

The relevance to you? I'd say the inventors of the USP were absolutely right, in principle, to acknowledge that all persuasive communication needs to present a competitive case; and that, further, when an obvious point of difference doesn't exist, it's up to the communicators to search until they find one.

Where they went wrong was in applying this principle over-literally. They believed that the product itself would, if scrutinised closely enough, always yield a USP. Through modern eyes, this looks absurd. We're perfectly well aware that, in many areas, differences between products are negligible going on non-existent.

And yet we still form preferences, and make choices. Based on what? At this point, we risk a lengthy and tedious diversion down the twisty and overgrown track that leads to an Understanding of the Theory of Brands. But I think we can spare ourselves that. For our purposes here, it's enough to observe that, when there's little or nothing between products, we choose the one that talks to us in the voice we find most engaging.

The USP is dead, long live the CP!

So let's agree to abandon the USP as unworkable, and replace it with what I'm going to call the CP, or Competitive Promise. By that, I mean a clear statement of why whatever you have to sell has an edge over the competition (whatever form that may take). Unlike a USP, this usually won't be based upon a single measurable, factual point of difference. Instead, a CP will often be a synthesis of substance and style. What you have to offer your reader may not, strictly speaking, be unique; but the combination of what you have to offer and how you offer it may be enough to tip the balance in your favour.

An example? For once, having numerous children is about to prove rather handy. Because, as I'm trying to work on this, my elder daughter Laura is pestering me about a letter she's writing. She's going to university in about six weeks' time, and she urgently needs to earn some money before then. Yesterday, she called into our local branch of Borders bookshops, and they told her to drop them a CV together with a covering letter explaining what she feels she has to offer them.

What does Laura have to offer Borders? Suppressing a father's blind partisanship, I'd have to say nothing unique. There are loads of bright, personable, impoverished students out there, looking for a not-too-taxing way of making some money before term begins. But she does have at least one competitive advantage: she does genuinely love books and reading – not something every 19-year-old can say. And, even by the standards of today's socially adept young, she is exceptionally confident and outgoing in her dealings with people (as the part-time and voluntary jobs on her CV suggest).

So what is the CP on which she should base her letter? Something like:

A book-lover who gets a buzz out of dealing with people.

Or, to spell out the promise more explicitly:

Hiring me will be good for your business because ... I've got the people skills, and I know my E M Forster from my J K Rowling.

Let's be clear, I'm not suggesting that these are the words Laura should use; just that this is what she should set out to communicate. It isn't, to be honest, an immensely strong Competitive Promise: if she has a rival for the job who used to work in a bookshop on Saturdays, then she's unlikely to be the successful candidate. But, working with the material available, it's about the best she can do. And if she can find the right words to bring this CP to life for the reader – to make herself sound as bright and lively and literate as she claims to be – then she might be in with a chance.

All of which means, as you may have noticed, that I've come full circle. I started this chapter by talking about the importance of how you write in influencing your reader, her response and the result; half way through, I turned my attention to the importance of what you write. And here I am, almost at the end of the chapter, concluding that, in the vast majority of persuasive writing, how and what you write can't possibly be separated. And so, finally, that brings us to ...

The rousing call to action

Do you know what I mean by that phrase? It's the bit at the end of an ad that says something like, 'Hurry down to your local XYZ store today, while this offer lasts' or 'Call us today on the number below to find out more'.

In the snootier, more self-important advertising agencies – the kind where the copywriters all think they are Quentin Tarantino, and they refer to TV ads for toilet cleaner as 'films' – such things are rather frowned upon. Putting the phone number or web address in bold type ruins the minimalist perfection of the art director's lay-out.

But I think a nice, clear call to action hardly ever goes amiss. Provided you're polite, what possible harm can there be in telling your reader what you would like her to do next, and how she should go about it?

Anyway, that's all I have to say about the general principles of good persuasive writing. To find out more about how to apply them in practice, simply turn the page and read on.

Go on, do it right now.

Section Two

A persuasive writing A to Z

A

adjectives

Here comes a sweeping statement. Good persuasive writers don't rely on adjectives.

Like most sweeping statements, that one needs a bit of qualifying. Of course, it would be impossible to write without using adjectives. Absurd, too, since they lend colour, variety and precision to otherwise lifeless nouns.

But when you are trying to persuade a reader to see things from your point of view, adjectives are very rarely the best tool for the job. Why? Because when you describe a car as exhilarating, an investment opportunity as remarkable, or a holiday destination as unforgettable, you are telling your reader what you think. She may not agree with you. In fact, since most people prefer to make up their own minds, she probably won't.

Much harder, but far more effective than reaching for a shop-worn adjective, is to tell your reader something about the car, the investment opportunity, the holiday destination that will lead her to draw the desired conclusion for herself.

Obvious? Perhaps. But it's amazing how often writers with something to sell cram their paragraphs full of superfluous, annoying, useless, redundant, otiose, counter-productive adjectives.

alliteration

Best before: Beowulf. Beware.

and

OK, let's get this straight once and for all: it isn't wrong to start a sentence with 'and'. And it never has been.

If you don't believe me, you can look it up in *Fowler's English Usage*, probably the most widely respected reference work on 'correct' English.

What if you don't believe Fowler? Well, in that case, I'd suggest you refer to William Shakespeare, Charles Dickens, Jane Austen, the author of the King James Bible, this year's Man Booker Prize winner or the editor of any of our national newspapers. Because throughout the history of written English, good writers – virtually without exception – have routinely and unapologetically started sentences with 'and'.

And on the other side of the argument? Who exactly are the authorities denouncing this 'incorrect' practice? Er ... well, nobody really. Whenever I ask people where they learnt this rule, they tell me they vaguely remember hearing it from a teacher in the early 1970s.

So that's a bit of a dilemma, then. Who to trust on a matter of good written English: Miss Hotchkiss late of Elmgrove Primary or every good writer since time began? Hmm, tricky.

And while we're on the subject, exactly the same applies to 'but'.

anger

It's fine to write when you're angry. In fact, I'd warmly recommend it as the best possible way of sorting out why something has upset you, clarifying your own position, and generally letting off steam.

So next time you're seriously disgruntled about something, by all means, sit down and write. But, whatever you do, just don't click on 'print' or 'send'. Because, almost without exception, anything written in hot blood will fail as persuasive writing – for the very simple reason that, when the red mist descends, it's impossible to see clearly either your reader or the result you are trying to achieve.

Leave it overnight, and read it again in the morning …
There, glad you didn't send it now, aren't you?

apostrophe

The apostrophe? Im sorry to say its probably on its way out.

Im sorry about it for two reasons, I suppose. Firstly, because I do believe that apostrophes can be useful in helping writers to make their meaning clear. And secondly, if Im honest, because being one of the very small minority of the population who knows how to use them correctly gives me a rather enjoyable sense of smug superiority.

But the truth is, the case for the apostrophes continued existence just isnt quite strong enough. In probably 98 out of 100 cases, the writers meaning is perfectly clear to an averagely intelligent reader without the help of one of those intrusive and fiddly little squiggles.

So Id be willing to bet that that in 50 years time the apostrophe will be dead and buried. But thats OK, because by then, so will I.

archipelago

Gorgeous, isn't it? Go on, say it aloud ... let the syllables dance a samba with your tongue. Undoubtedly one of my all-time favourite words – though, sadly, I very rarely get a chance to use it.

But it's important for writers to love words for their own sake.

argument

Right, let's have an argument. No, not the taking-it-in-turns-to-point-out-each-other's-glaringly-obvious-shortcomings kind of argument, so familiar to all of us in long-term relation-ships. I mean the kind that forms the basis of every successful piece of persuasive writing.

Actually, there are a number of different terms that we could use here. STORY is a good one, because it suggests the way that a continuous thread carries the reader through from beginning to end, wanting to know 'what happens next'.

Structure is pretty close to my meaning, too, referring to the way a good piece of writing is built around a sturdy framework that holds everything together. And journalists talk about looking for an angle (at least, they do in films about journalists); a way of approaching a pile of facts, opinion and information that helps the reader to understand what it is that she is seeing.

But I prefer argument, for two main reasons.

First, because it brings to mind the way a lawyer argues a case in court – which is clearly the closest analogy in the world of work to what a good persuasive writer does. We don't make things up; we don't try to deceive anyone. We just listen to our client's version of events, probe gently (or not so gently) to clarify any inconsistencies … then construct the strongest, most watertight case we can on the client's behalf.

And second, because very often, the best persuasive writing does actually involve picking a quarrel.

Who with? Anyone putting forward an opposing point of view. In the world of professional persuasive writing, of course, that often means the competition: ('According to Brand X, their kippers/spark plugs/computer games are the freshest/longest lasting/most entertaining; but when you try ours, you'll find out what fresh/long lasting/entertaining really means.')

But, perhaps even more often, the quarrel is with the reader. That's to say, good persuasive writers use their understanding of the reader to construct an argument that directly addresses her attitudes or preconceptions:

'So you think you're too young to worry about a pension?'

'If you think one low calorie cheese spread is pretty much like another, take the Cheeso-Challenge and we'll prove you wrong.'

'You don't have to be boring to train as an accountant. No, really, you don't.'

For me, persuasive writing is always more enjoyable – and far less likely to be become BORING – when it sets out to change the reader's mind; or, at least, to give her some good reasons to reconsider the way she currently thinks or feels.

Anyone care to argue?

B

because

Do you ever get completely stuck when you're writing something? I do, and it's nearly always because I've lost sight of the basics: what I want my reader to think, feel or do; and the most compelling reason why she should.

So sometimes, I find it helpful to sum up what I'm trying to say, however long and complex it may be, in one shortish sentence, containing the word 'because'. For example:

'Sell your home through XYZ estate agents because we know the market better and will get you a better price.'

'Give us the contract because you can rely on us not to screw it up like your previous supplier.'

'Answer my Lonely Hearts ad because I have a very good sense of humour.'

(being) boring

The second worst crime a persuasive writer can commit, after treating the reader like an idiot.

brackets

A lot of people (I can't think why) accuse me of over-using brackets. (Well, perhaps I can.) But I'm unrepentant. (Think why, I mean.)

For me, brackets are one of the most important items in a writer's tool-box. (Like a Philips screwdriver.)

Why? Because brackets enable a writer to add something that explains, expands or comments upon what goes before (and sometimes also what follows) without interrupting the flow. (So the test of whether they are used properly is to remove the bits in brackets and see whether what you are left with still makes sense.)

Think of it as another voice, chipping in with a comment on what the main 'speaker' is saying. This works best, I think, when the second voice is a humorous one, which undermines, or gives an unexpected twist to what has gone before. Like this line I recently wrote for a press ad, for example:

Free seeds with your ABC Garden catalogue. (We admit, it's a sow-sow offer.)

For me a PUN that bad could only work in brackets.

bullet points

Bullet points are OK, provided they're not:

- over-used
- mis-used
- for example, when people use them to include something that doesn't follow on from the previous bullet points
- just because
- they think it makes it 'easier to read'
- Wrong!
- It doesn't

C

claims

Lindsay Camp is the world's greatest lover.

Bad example, actually – because I think that's pretty much beyond dispute. But, in most cases, the problem with making big claims is that people won't believe them until they have seen some kind of proof.

Good writers provide it. If a hotel is 'the ultimate in luxury', they will tell us how many metres wide the sunken baths are, or which species of silkworm is responsible for the sheets. If a car is 'the most technologically advanced in its class', they will be sure to mention a few of the gizmos that make it so.

Bad writers do the opposite. That's to say, they don't merely fail to substantiate their claims; they actually disprove them.

You want me to believe, for example, that you are 'a law firm with a difference'. Then how come you're droning on, like every law firm since time began, about being totally committed to client-focused solutions? A financial services company that 'speaks my language'? Then why do you assume that I know what an ISA is?

Never make a claim unless you are sure you can make it stand up when it matters. That's Lindsay Camp's advice.

cliché

So what exactly is a cliché? A phrase that was once fresh but is now rapidly going stale. Let's take a random example:

thinking outside the box

It's hard to imagine, but there probably was a time when this sounded dynamic and unexpected. People reading or hearing it may have paused for a moment to consider its implications, conjuring up a mental image of themselves inside a box, but bravely refusing to allow their thinking to be restricted by it.

Now it just sounds tired and flat. In fact, the phrase has come to carry the exact opposite of its original meaning. When people urge us to think outside the box, we immediately suspect that their own thinking is lazy and unoriginal.

So what's wrong with clichés? We've already answered that above. Language that's no longer fresh loses its power and even its meaning. More specifically, it loses its capacity to surprise. When we start to read a cliché, we know exactly what's coming next:

the pursuit of ... excellence
barking up ... the wrong tree
singing off ... the same song-sheet
past its ... sell-by date
the dog's ... well, you get the idea

And when we feel that we know what's coming next, what possible reason can there be to continue reading?

cliché (2)

Saying that clichés should be avoided 'like the plague' has become a cliché. From now on, clichés should be avoided like the centre of town on a Saturday night.

concise

I've lost count of the number of briefing meetings I've been in where everyone present has been of the opinion that in this particular piece of communication, the text should be kept to a minimum. On the other hand, I can't remember a single occasion when the designer or the client has looked me in the eye and said, 'Lindsay, this time I think we need you to ramble on self-indulgently for as long as possible.'

So at least that's one thing everyone's agreed on. The fewer of those nasty confusing little words cluttering up the nice clean lay-out, the more effective the communication.

Like most nonsensical beliefs, this one contains at least a few shreds of common sense. In an age in which most people seem to measure their own worth by how over-worked they are, it's obviously a good idea not to waste anyone's time. And yes, while we're making concessions, it's true that any piece of writing can be condensed, and then condensed again. A 200-word executive summary of a lengthy report? No problem. The key message of the New

Testament in three words? Love thy neighbour.
But, of course, unless a piece of writing is full of padding, you inevitably lose something in the process of cutting it. What you lose will vary, but may include any of the following: wit, intelligence, sparkle, pace, coherence, clarity, telling detail ... oh yes, and the reader's attention.

Good writers have a strong sense of how long their material will sustain the interest of their readers, and of how many words they need in order to tell a story as powerfully as possible.

A four-word summary of the above? Shorter isn't necessarily better.

content

Content matters more than STYLE. In fact, if what you're saying is strong enough, how you say it hardly matters at all. 'Free £20 notes. Please take one.' See? No discernible style at all.

conversational

Quite often, people describe my writing as conversational. Sometimes, more disparagingly, they call it 'chatty'.

What do they mean? Eavesdrop on the average office or pub conversation and what you'll hear doesn't usually sound much like good writing. ('So he turns round to me, and says, 'You what?' And I'm like, whoa, don't even go there ... ')

So I could take 'conversational' as an insult; a not very subtle way of suggesting that my writing is incoherent, repetitive, clumsily expressed.

But actually – being a cheery, optimistic soul – I prefer to put a much more positive interpretation on it. Because for me, writing 'conversationally' means two things, both good.

First, it means writing pretty much as I would speak (assuming I knew the subject back to front). No unnecessary long words. No lifeless corporate-speak ('optimising' this or 'prioritising' that.) None of those archaic-sounding phrases ('in the eventuality of'; 'lest it be thought that') that people use to make their writing sound more important. No rambling, convoluted sentences.

Second, and even more important, if my writing is conversational, that implies I'm talking to someone. Bad writing doesn't do this. It talks to itself. It drones on, interminably, like a party bore – telling you what it wants to say, utterly unconcerned with what you might be interested to hear.

I believe rather passionately that the single most important principle of good writing is to remember that somebody else is always there, reading and responding to what you have written.

I wonder if you agree?

D

disinterested

Once, disinterested meant, roughly, not having an axe to grind. If you acted disinterestedly, you did something without considering whether you stood to gain by it.

It doesn't mean that any more. Now, when people use the word, it usually means the same as uninterested – i.e. bored by, not giving a toss about. As in, 'I'm not eating there again; the waiter was totally disinterested'.

Personally, I think that's a pity. I still prefer the original meaning. But, like the evolution of a species, the way a living language develops isn't something you can argue with. Once a word is generally used in a particular sense, it's too late to bleat about it really meaning something else.

The problem, of course, is knowing when that point has been reached. Some, myself included, might still be prepared to argue the toss over 'disinterested'. But in other cases, it's clear-cut: the original meaning is as obsolete as the electric typewriter. Just imagine anyone, for example, trying to use 'gay' in any sense other than the one it has acquired over the last 10 or 15 years.

For persuasive writers, the judge and jury in these cases must be the reader. I may have my own opinion about what a word ought to mean; but if I insist on using it in that way when I know that for you it means something else, then I am wilfully making it difficult for you to understand me.

Not something a buxom[5] writer would ever wish to do.

E

editing

Something that ~~really~~ good persuasive writers never stop doing.

empathy

The single most important attribute of any good persuasive writer; the ability to see the world – and what you've written – through your reader's eyes.

emphasis

Sometimes, when you have something **REALLY *important*** to say, it's tempting to use EVERY POSSIBLE MEANS to make sure your reader doesn't *miss the point*!!!

[5]Before it came to mean pleasingly plump, 'buxom' had a number of senses, including kindly, gracious and obliging.

But don't. Most people don't like being shouted at. And the louder you shout, very often the less they actually hear.

In a well-constructed sentence, it should be clear to the reader where the emphasis lies. But if you feel you really need to use italics, underlining, emboldening and other such devices, you'll find they are much more effective used *sparingly*.

engaging

I love and therefore massively over-use this word. For me, it perfectly captures the most important quality of good persuasive writing: the way it puts itself out to meet the reader on her own terms.

Is it engaging? Then it will almost certainly be persuasive.

exaggeration

When I first started making my living as a persuasive writer, I would have said that exaggeration was always a mistake; a sure way to lose the TRUST of the reader.

Now, several hundred years later, I think it can occasionally be quite effective.

F

fewer

Just in case you're interested, it should be **fewer** when you're talking about the number of something – for example, goals, brilliant ideas, or liquorice allsorts.

And it should be *less* when you're talking about the amount of something – for example, money, cheese, or human happiness.

So: to lose weight, eat less cheese and fewer liquorice allsorts.

Or: he scored fewer goals this season, so he deserves to be paid less money.

Does this distinction really matter? It does to me. But I realise that I'm probably in a minority.

In fact, I suspect these days most people couldn't care fewer.

flow

Good writing just does, doesn't it? Flow, I mean. One sentence segues seamlessly into the next. Each paragraph picks up where its predecessor left off. You start reading at the beginning and, before you know it, you're at the end.

Partly, this is a matter of technique: good writers choose their words carefully, vary the rhythm of their sentences and add colour – an apt simile or metaphor, perhaps – in order to carry the reader along with them.

But, mostly, the best persuasive writing has that feeling of unstoppable forward momentum because of the way the ideas flow. It's almost nothing to do with mere verbal dexterity. The skill involved is the ability to construct a compelling argument, and then to present it in the form of a single, coherent thought process – in which every word, every sentence, every paragraph serves the same broader purpose, and falls naturally into place.

f***

If I write the word fuck, you may or may not be mildly shocked. It depends, I suppose, on a number of factors: the context, what age you are, how strict your parents were; that kind of thing.

But if I write f***, what happens then? Are your delicate sensibilities, as some newspapers still suppose, protected by those asterisks?

Of course not. Because you fill in the blanks. Assuming you know the word, it's impossible not to. That's to say, instead of merely allowing your eye to pass swiftly over a word you may find offensive, you actively participate in the 'publication' of that word.

Writers make marks on screen or paper; readers supply their meaning. And anyone who tells you otherwise is talking b******s.

G

generosity

I love the idea that when we communicate with other people we should consider ourselves to be giving them something; and that the more we give, the greater the chance that our communication will achieve its goal.

What is it that the reader receives from good persuasive writing? Something that she finds interesting, useful or enjoyable.

Think of it as another test you can apply to what you have written: 'Does this piece of writing give my reader anything – and, if so, have I been as generous as possible?'

grammar

How much grammar does a good persuasive writer need to know?

At first glance, this seems like quite a tricky question. After all, who is to say whether a thorough understanding of the

subjunctive mood is optional, desirable or indispensable?
And how are we to gauge the importance of knowing the
difference between a preposition and a conjunction?

But actually, there's a simple answer. As a persuasive writer,
you need to know as much grammar as your reader – or
perhaps just a little more. Otherwise, she will be continually
bumping into your hanging pronouns or tripping over your
dangling participles.

And you wouldn't want that, would you?

humour

I'm going to tell you my favourite joke; but I'm afraid you
probably won't find it funny, unless you're a writer. (And
even then, there's a good chance you may not.)

It's a true story. A few years back, university lecturers were
up in arms about something or other. They held a protest
rally. A picture appeared on the front page of the newspaper;
in the foreground, a large home made banner bearing the
rousing slogan:

Rectify the Anomaly!

Hysterical, no? Well, it is to me; tears are coursing down my sallow and sunken cheeks as I write.

Why do I find it so funny? I'm pretty sure the answer is incongruity.

What do you expect to see on protest banners? 'More pay now!' perhaps. Maybe 'Nuclear power? No thanks!!!' Or even 'Kill the pigs!' In this context, the musty academic ring of 'Rectify the Anomaly!' is ludicrously out of place. We picture a mild-mannered philosophy tutor getting so worked up that he can contain himself no longer, and reaches for his felt-tips …

So, lesson one: incongruity – putting things where they are out of place – is a rich source of humour in writing, as in life.

And lesson two (based upon your stony face when I recounted the joke above): never forget that humour is highly subjective.

I

impact

I'm looking at an ad for a building society. It shows the rear view of a naked, shaven-headed man who appears to have a large number of sharp rectangular objects – razor blades perhaps – embedded under his skin.

It undeniably has great impact. Anyone flicking idly through this magazine would, like me, pause for a moment to take a closer look. And given that the vast majority of expensively produced ads are totally ignored by most people, that has to be a good thing, doesn't it?

Well, no actually. Because the image is a scary and disturbing one; the stuff of nightmares; a bit David Lynch. And, despite some leaden word play (something to do with 'getting under your skin'), it's utterly irrelevant to what the building society is hoping to communicate. All it achieves is to make me shudder slightly, before turning the page.

Often, persuasive writing needs to get noticed, in order to have a chance of being read; but if, in gaining your reader's attention, you lose her sympathy, you almost certainly won't achieve the result you're after.

intelligence

Something which, unlike KNOWLEDGE, you should always assume your reader possesses.

irony

Among the most pressing questions facing our society today are how we define irony and whether it's a good idea for writers to use it.

Actually, of course, these questions aren't very pressing at all. But that's irony for you: saying the opposite of what we really mean in order to achieve a particular effect – usually, gently humorous.

Incidentally, don't allow yourself to be swayed on this by the beautiful and highly talented Alanis Morissette, whose song 'Ironic' suggested such examples of irony as '10,000 spoons when all you need is a knife' and 'a free ride when you've already paid'. Wrong, Ms Morissette: you may have sold 35 million CDs worldwide, but what you're talking about there is Sod's Law; not the same thing, at all.

For a better example of what irony is, and how it works, let's turn to Jane Austen:

> It is a truth universally acknowledged that a single man in possession of a good fortune must be in want of a wife.

Well, no, it isn't. In fact, we know that the reverse is true:

that rich men tend to be more than usually shy of commitment, and are far more likely to be pursued by potential wives than to feel themselves in want of one. And, knowing this, we – as readers – supply the writer's true, intended meaning.

Which is why irony is so important to good writers. Used well, it's just about the most powerful means there is of involving readers; persuading them to 'participate' in the experience of reading, rather than merely sitting back and letting the words wash over them.

A note on the difference between irony and sarcasm

Actually, they are very nearly the same. Sarcasm, too, involves saying the opposite of what we really mean. But sarcasm is irony's mean-spirited sibling; its intention is not to amuse and engage, but to wound. For example, 'I seriously think you should consider a career as a rocket scientist' or 'No, really, you look fantastic in those pink PVC trousers.'

J

jargon

Something else we can all agree on: jargon is a very, very
bad thing and should be avoided at all costs when we're
writing.

But what do we actually mean by that?

Consider these words and phrases: layout, embossed,
kerning, sans serif font, percentage tint.

If you're a graphic designer, you certainly won't think they
are jargon. They are all an indispensable part of your
everyday working vocabulary. (Imagine having to say 'a sort
of printed writing without any knobbly bits on the letters'
instead of 'a sans serif font'.)

But to the vast majority of the British public, most of the
words and phrases above would be a bit obscure, if not
completely baffling.

As ever with writing, it's all about the reader. There's no such
thing as jargon; only one person's everyday language
mistakenly used in conversation with somebody else.

jargon (2)

Actually, of course, there is another kind of jargon; the kind I think of as management-consultant-speak, although other professions have their own versions.

What we're talking about here is disunintentionally obfuscatory verbalisation procedures – i.e. using obscure language with the specific aim of making what you are saying sound mysterious and complicated to 'outsiders', thereby justifying your enormous fees.

Unlike the first kind of jargon – which is a very, very bad thing to be avoided at all costs – this kind is morally repugnant, and should be severely punished.

joke

How do you turn a duck into a soul singer? Put it in the oven until its bill withers.

(Barely relevant joke included on the grounds that the punchline depends on whether or not there is an APOSTROPHE in 'its'.)

K

knocking

… as in 'knocking copy', a phrase which sounds rather archaic these days. But it's still worth a mention – and not just because I've been struggling to think of anything beginning with K.

It refers, of course, to the kind of advertising in which the product is directly compared to a named competitor, to the latter's detriment. On the whole, advertisers avoid doing this for two main reasons – one good, one less so.

The good reason is that it can be very difficult indeed to make fair and appropriate comparisons. And if your target audience knows (or suspects) that the comparison being made is unfair or inappropriate, the ad may well prove counter-productive. (I could, to take an extreme example, tell you that a Ford Fiesta does more miles to the gallon than a Ferrari, but you probably wouldn't be impressed.)

The other reason advertisers shy away from directly attacking their competitors is the quite reasonable fear that they may retaliate. In most markets, a kind of gentleman's agreement not to name names is in force.

It's important to recognise, though, that all advertising aims to knock down the competition, whether or not it's mentioned by name. The ad I write may present the case for buying XYZ spark plugs, but the one you read is just as much to do with why you shouldn't buy the inferior ABC product you've been using for years.

And the same applies to all persuasive writing. Of course, you probably won't refer to a named competitor ('Give the job to me, not that Neanderthal half-wit Geoff Robson'). You may not even realise that what you are trying to sell has competition. But whenever you set out to use words to influence anyone, in any way, they always have other options. So every piece of persuasive writing must, in effect, be knocking copy.

knowledge

Something which, unlike INTELLIGENCE, you should never assume your reader possesses.

L

letter

Dear All,
Oh god!

Christmas again already! Doesn't time fly? Especially for

You know why your heart sinks when you receive one of those

all us here in Little Snittington, where 2006 has been

circular letters, don't you? Of course you do. It's because the

among the most incident-packed years in living memory.

people who write them aren't really writing to you. They're

January saw Jenny taking part in her first gymkhana

writing to the old school friend who emigrated to Canada in

and Marcus selected for the first XV, and a very proud

1987; the bloke they used to share an office with; the aged

Mum and Dad shouting themselves hoarse (or should

relative who never forgets to send birthday and Christmas cards;

that be 'horse'?!?) on the sidelines! But soon afterwards,

that really nice couple they met in Turkey a few years back ... in

one of several brushes with the National Health Service

fact, they're writing to everyone they can't be arsed to keep in

occurred when poor old Derek's rickety knee flared up,

touch with properly. So, of course, it's impossible for them to

necessitating exploratory surgery, and three nights in

write anything that might conceivably be of interest to you.

hospital. All well now, fingers crossed!!! The crocuses

However many people may actually receive it, a letter is always

were glorious this year – and, speaking of the garden, we

one-to-one communication. Any letter that fails to connect with

installed a specially attractive new water feature (shades

you, the reader, on this level, isn't really a letter at all. It's just

of Charlie Dimmock!!) in time for Easter. Speaking of

another piece of junk mail. So feel free to bin it, unread.

loaded language

I believe that the relationship between a persuasive writer and a reader should be honest and open. Why? Because if I make you feel for a single moment that I am trying to dupe or hoodwink you, then I will almost certainly lose your trust for ever – along with any hope of winning you round to my point of view.

But not everyone shares this belief. And there are a number of linguistic dirty tricks writers can press into service, one of which is the use of loaded language. That's to say, words or phrases that look 'neutral' but which actually carry a (sometimes controversial) hidden agenda.

As an example, let's consider one of the most heavily loaded phrases currently in frequent use: 'politically correct'. The first thing to recognise is that, despite appearing to be merely a description, it is in fact always derogatory. It's impossible for something or someone to be politically correct in a good way.

But what does it actually mean? My admittedly rather plonky definition would be something like: 'a phrase descriptive of actions or words that show an exaggerated concern for the interests of a minority group, in a way that offends the common sense of ordinary, decent people not belonging to that group'.

I hope you will agree that roughly captures it. But let's look at a few examples:

- A male manager being sacked for sexually harassing a young female employee
- A major political party using reverse discrimination to ensure the election of more female MPs
- A nursery school banning the nursery rhyme 'Baa Baa Black Sheep' on the grounds of negative stereotyping
- The phrase 'differently abled' being used to replace 'disabled' or 'handicapped'

Unless you have pretty extreme views, you probably wouldn't regard all of the above as examples of political correctness. A few (or possibly even all of them) may well seem like perfectly reasonable behaviour to you. You and I might or might not agree about which.

But that's the point about loaded language. Its aim is to take away the reader's right to dissent – by disguising the writer's own opinion or belief as something acknowledged to be true by common consent.

As I'm quite certain any right-minded person would agree.

logic

A vital ingredient of good persuasive writing, though almost entirely useless without an added dash of EMPATHY.

M

Malapropisms

Never use a word unless you're 100% certain of its meaning. We've all been tempted to do it – in order to make ourselves sound more grandiloquent and meretricious.

But it nearly always turns out crapulously.

N

negative

Quite often, I come across people who believe it's wrong to write anything 'negative'.

They're not entirely mistaken. Think, for example, of our old friend Gerald Ratner who famously described the jewellery sold by his high street stores as 'crap'. That's pretty negative, isn't it? And I don't think anyone would want to make a case for it as an effective piece of persuasive communication. (Least of all Mr Ratner whose business went bust soon afterwards.)

But, of course, a 'negative' can be much more POSITIVE than that. And I hope you won't think me horribly conceited if I illustrate how with a line which I recently wrote for a local firm of estate agents:

XYZ Estate Agents. The relatively painless way to sell your home.

There is a negative aspect to it, I can't deny; an admission that, even with the help of the world's finest estate agents, selling property nearly always involves a degree of pain. But, for me (and for the client in question, happily), the candour of that admission is very winning; much more appealing than, say:

XYZ Estate Agents. Going the extra mile to deliver a smoother move.

So far, then, we've seen a negative-negative and a positive-negative; and yes, there is also such a thing as a negative-positive:

Incredibly good looking guy, loaded, Mensa IQ, VGSOH, wltm ...

Obviously a man with a very positive self-image; but if you were scanning the Lonely Hearts column, you probably wouldn't fancy going on a blind date with him.

What matters in persuasive writing is not what the writer puts in, but what the reader takes out. No?

nuance

Lovely word; nothing else quite captures the meaning, does it?

numbers

Three points about using numbers in persuasive writing:

1 It's a good idea, especially when you're making any kind of CLAIM. 'At XYZ Health Foods we stock 27 different types of muesli' is much more convincing than 'At XYZ Health Foods we stock a comprehensive range of mueslis'.

2 For some reason, single digit numbers are traditionally written as words (one, two, three), whereas anything in double figures upwards is shown in figures (10 not ten; 2,657,239,142,230,255,987 not two gazillion etc). Does this matter to your reader? Probably not. Just thought I'd mention it.

3 Sorry, there is no three; but scientific research shows that three points always look at least 50% better than two.

O

off-putting

Usually, persuasive writing aims to attract. But that isn't always its sole aim. Quite often, putting off the wrong people is hardly less important than seducing the right ones.

Take this ad, scrawled on the back of an envelope, in my local newsagent's window:

> Do you dislike your flatmates? Do they perhaps smell. Our friend Derek is going to Hong Kong to work hard for a dodgy company so we have a spare room in our lovely house.
>
> Would you like to share with three nice boys (two French) and one girl? No townies! Hippys OK. Students ~~maybe~~ OK. Help us grow flowers in our garden would be nice! There will be a test.

Even if my wife throws me out tomorrow, I probably won't be replying to that ad. But that's what makes it so good. The last thing our happy, hippy housemates want is dozens of phone calls from homeless old fogeys, squares, members of the Countryside Alliance, trainee solicitors or, indeed, townies.

opening

A good one grabs you by the throat. It can do this in all kinds of ways, but a really effective opening sentence will always observe one fundamental principle of good writing. That the reader owes you nothing. Love letters aside, no piece of writing has a divine right to be read.

In fact, good writers should always start with the opposite assumption: that the reader has other, more pressing things to do. From the outset, the biggest challenge is to give her a reason to read, and continue reading.

One lapse – into irrelevance, unintelligibility or plain dullness – and they'll be gone.

Still with me? Phew!

opening (2)

~~I always spend ages over the first sentence of anything I'm writing – and with good reason, since my opening lines will determine whether my reader remains my reader.~~

~~But i~~It's amazing how often a brilliant opening sentence or paragraph turns out to be completely redundant; nothing more than an obstacle that the reader has to scramble over before reaching anything of any real interest or value.

over-familiarity

Here's the opening of a letter my wife recently received, inviting her to subscribe to a well-known American business journal:

> Your career isn't just about money, is it?
>
> I didn't think so. It's about something deeper.
>
> Something so central to your core, to what makes you tick, that you can't imagine living without it.
>
> It's about leadership. Having your say. Making things happen. Putting your stamp on the future.

Hateful, isn't it? And here's why: it's grotesquely over-familiar. These people, remember, have never met my wife. Beyond her name, address and job description, they know precisely nothing about her. Yet here they are telling her what is 'central to her core'. The bludgeoning sycophancy of that last paragraph positively demands the response, 'No, actually, I'm only working to pay for my crack habit ... '

As persuasive writers, we want to win over our readers. We want them to trust us and, very often, we want them to like us.

But lay off the smarm, that's my advice. Though I'm sure that someone as discerning and perceptive as you would never make such a foolish mistake.

P

paragraphs

You know how in ads virtually every sentence forms a new paragraph?

Annoying, isn't it?

The assumption that, unless the text is broken down into teeny weeny morsels, you won't be capable of digesting it.

I don't know about you, but I find that a bit patronising.

After all, I read newspapers.

Magazines.

Even books.

All of which quite often contain paragraphs consisting of several sentences – and I don't have any particular trouble reading them. So no, I definitely wouldn't recommend you to adopt the single-sentence-per-para approach. But, having said that, it is important to bear in mind how the piece you're writing will look on the page; and I think it is true that a large expanse of densely packed text can look a little daunting to many readers. So, on the whole, unless I was writing for a highly literate reader, a university professor perhaps, I'd very rarely write a paragraph longer than this one.

polysyllables

Not long ago, I gave a talk about persuasive writing to a group of talented young designers. As usual on such occasions, I got some easy laughs by administering a sound kicking to words like UTILISE, beverage and commence. (Use, drink and start, of course.)

But afterwards, one of the talented young designers approached me and accused me – very politely – of dumbing down the English language. I was genuinely shocked. I thought I'd made it very clear that my beef was with the unnecessary use of long 'important sounding' words in place of shorter, more workaday ones. She, equally clearly, had heard me saying 'good writers always avoid using long words'.

So let me make it as plain as I possibly can. There is absolutely nothing wrong with using long words – or, indeed, any word at all – provided there is nothing questionable about your motivation for doing so. Are you trying to impress the reader? Are you trying to make something sound better than it really is? Are you trying to obscure your meaning?

If so, then stop it. Right now. Find a shorter word, and start showing your reader a little RESPECT.

But if, on the other hand, you're planning to use a long word because it more precisely conveys your meaning, or because it's the only word that adequately captures a specific idea, or even because you think that a little verbal colour will give your reader pleasure ... then go ahead, and do it without hesitation.

Polysyllablise pertinently and unrepentantly.

positive

Of course, it's a well-known fact that two negatives make a positive. But I was surprised to read recently that, according to language experts, the opposite does not apply: that two positives can never make a negative.

Yeah, right.

PS

In the direct marketing/junk mail industry, they have all kinds of impressively scientific-sounding laws decreeing how to produce effective communications. It's a proven fact, for example, that repeating the special offer mentioned on page one a third of the way down page two, will increase response rates by over 40%. (Actually, I made that up, but you get the idea.)

Normally, I don't have much time for this kind of stuff. But there is one Golden Rule of Effective Direct Marketing that I tend to agree with: always remember that, when reading a letter, most people's eyes are drawn towards the postscript. In some cases, it may be all they read.

So it makes a lot of sense to use a PS to encapsulate the most important point in your letter.

Quite often, I write it first.

pun

What is it with writers and crap puns? The answer, I suppose, is that we love language and therefore enjoy playing with it – just as toddlers have a passion for puddles, and get a kick out of jumping into them.

But sometimes I really think we need to be given a good slap.

Two recent examples, chosen entirely at random. Exhibit A: a piece in a local magazine about the pleasures of flying kites. Headline? 'The kite stuff'. Exhibit B: an ad for low-cost wood laminate flooring. Headline? 'You'll be floored by our prices'.

In case A, I'd say the pun is entirely indefensible. It refers, presumably, to *The Right Stuff*, a book and also a film about the first American astronauts. There's no connection with kite-flying. The only justification is that 'right' rhymes with 'kite'.

Case B is slightly different. The word 'floor' is used in two senses: the literal one, and the metaphorical one of being so surprised as to be incapable of standing up. If we were feeling charitable, we might just about excuse this – on the grounds that a pun 'works' when it brings together two different meanings of a word, both of which have some relevance to the matter in hand.

But, unfortunately, there's more to it than that. In fact, a pun only works when it brings together two different meanings of a word, both of which have some relevance to the matter in hand, in a way that doesn't make readers feel they've been slapped in the face with a dead fish.

Next time you read a piece of writing full of clever double meanings, ask yourself do they add anything to the reader's understanding or enjoyment?

Or are they just the Puns of Navarone?

punctuation

Some people worry about punctuation but what I say is, as long as it's clear to the reader what you mean then it's no big deal.

Some people worry about punctuation; but what I say is, as long as it's clear to the reader what you mean, then it's no big deal.

Some people worry about punctuation – but what I say is, as long as it's clear to the reader what you mean, then it's no big deal.

Some people worry about punctuation but what I say is: 'As long as it's clear to the reader what you mean, then it's no big deal.'

Some people worry about punctuation. But what I say is – as long as it's clear to the reader what you mean, then it's no big deal.

To find out if it is, read what you've written aloud.

punctuation (2)

I wrote the above some time before Lynne Truss achieved the most surreal runaway success in recent publishing history with *Eats, Shoots and Leaves*.

On the face of it, this should stop me in my tracks – since Ms Trusses' (just kidding, Lynne) book argues for a 'zero tolerance approach to punctuation'. And the fact that several billion people have bought into this would seem to put my far more permissive attitude firmly in the wrong.

But, while I'm a little baffled by the *ESL* phenomenon, I'm unrepentant. Because, as far as persuasive writing is concerned, there is simply no room for pedantry, in relation to punctuation – or anything else.

Don't misunderstand me: I'm not suggesting that anything goes. True, I don't think that good persuasive writers should be bound by an inflexible set of punctuation rules, but I do believe that they should use punctuation with the greatest care and consideration, and in a consistent manner, in the service of the reader.

Most of the time, this will mean observing a few widely accepted conventions – a full stop at the end of the sentence, that kind of thing. But, when we write persuasively, the only cast-iron rule is that every mark we make on the page or screen must make it more rather than less likely that the reader will be won round to our point of view.

Q

questions

So what's wrong with rhetorical questions? Absolutely nothing. In fact, I use them quite a bit.

Why? Because I think that they can help a writer pull off one of the most difficult tricks there is.

Which is? Giving the reader a voice.

What does that mean? It means that rhetorical questions in a piece of writing can, in effect, represent the reader. Think of them as interruptions on the reader's behalf – asking for clarification, or pointing out a possible flaw in the writer's argument, for example.

But how does the writer know what the reader wants to 'ask'? That's the hard part. If the question doesn't reflect what the reader might want to know at that particular moment, then the device will quickly start to sound contrived and irritating. But getting inside the reader's mind is what good writing is all about.

So, used well, rhetorical questions are a way of making a monologue into a two-way conversation? Something like that.

But is it possible to overdo them? Apparently.

R

repetition

Yesterday my daughter came home from school and told me that it's wrong to use **and** twice in the same sentence.

This brought to mind that old story about the packaging designer being asked by the client, a well-known manufacturer of baby food, to leave more space on the label between Cow and and and and and Gate. But it also seriously annoyed me. Because what, in sanity's name, could possibly be wrong with, say:

Mum and Dad took Lily and her dog to the park.

Repetition is only a problem if it's likely to bother the reader. For example, if I used the word repetition repeatedly in the same sentence, the repetition of repetition would certainly start to grate. So I wouldn't.

But, of course, I might very well repeat myself deliberately for effect. And I'm sure any estate agent who has ever summed up the three most important factors in selling a property would agree.

respect

What good persuasive writers always show for their readers.

rhythm

Difficult to explain, this. But worth a try, because good writing does have a sense of rhythm, a dum-di-dum-di-dum-di-dum quality that makes it more pleasurable to read.

For example, look at these two phrases, and try if you can to forget their meaning:

Trousers for women
Trousers for men

Say them aloud, one after the other. Now say them the other way round. Which way round sounds better, more satisfying, more 'conclusive'?

For me, it's clearly the way I've written them above. Why? Because it ends on a stressed syllable: men. Whereas the other way round, the final sound we hear is the unstressed ending of women.

Or to put it another way, *dum-di-di dum-di, dum-di-di dum* sounds an awful lot better to me than, *dum-di-di dum, dum-di-di dum-di*.

I wonder if you can hear the difference?

S

self-deprecation

Here's the best bit of persuasive writing I've read recently:

We're still hopeless at pack design.

Perhaps a bit of context might help. The sentence appears on the website of a well-known design consultancy. It comes towards the end of a section in which they explain what kind of work they do, and what they believe their strengths to be. They are, apparently, very good indeed at all types of corporate literature, pretty hot at web design, excellent at annual reports ... but still hopeless at pack design.

It's totally disarming, isn't it? Just when we're expecting an unbroken catalogue of success, a bracing blast of candid self-criticism. We're instantly won over: they sound so nice and so human. And yet, underlying those warm, cuddly virtues, we sense a steely self-confidence in their willingness to admit to anything less than all-round perfection. 'These guys must be fantastic designers to get away with that,' we find ourselves thinking.

Anyway, I wish I'd written that sentence, or one half as good. But, sadly, I've always been completely useless at self-deprecation.

sentence

How long should a sentence be? (6) I've always wondered, and the other day I found out, when I visited a website offering free advice to would-be copywriters. (21) Here's what it told me: '10 words per sentence is about right for press advertisements, while 15 word sentences suit direct mail and brochures. (24) Any sentence that exceeds 25 words will be difficult to follow'. (11)

Blimey! (1) Imagine how concerned I was to learn that I've been getting it wrong all these years. (16) Because, until now, I have hardly ever counted the number of words in a sentence I've written. (17)

Why not? (2) I'll give you three good reasons. (6)

1 Because the idea of a standard length that is 'about right' for sentences – in press ads, brochures, or anywhere else – is absurd. (22) Good writing has rhythm; it flows. (6) And one of the ways that writers achieve this is by using sentences of different lengths; a couple of longish ones, followed by a slightly shorter one, followed by a teeny weeny one. (33) That kind of thing. (4)

2 Anyway, what is a sentence? (5) Yes, of course, it's a unit of writing with a capital letter at the beginning and a full stop at the end. (22) But actually, where your sentences begin and end is very largely to do with your taste in punctuation; whether, for example, you prefer to use a semicolon or a full stop. (31) Chucking in more full stops and capital letters doesn't necessarily make your meaning clearer to your reader. (17)

3 Most of all, though, I find it gob-smackingly patronising to assert, without qualification, that any sentence of more than 25 words will be difficult to follow. (26) Why should it be, unless the reader is a young child or someone otherwise afflicted with serious literacy issues? (19)

Oh, all right, I suppose I will admit that there's a particle of common sense in advising inexperienced writers to avoid long, rambling sentences. (24) But only a very small particle. (6) Because, if a sentence is properly constructed, carefully worded and – most important of all – contains something of real interest to the reader, there's absolutely no reason why it can't go on for, oh, as many as 38 words. (38)

simile

When I was at primary school, shortly after the Crimean War, we were given lists of similes to learn, and tested on them regularly. 'As black as … ' the teacher would say; and those of us who had done our homework obediently scribbled 'night'.

For each simile, there was one correct answer. If, instead of 'night' I had written 'a witch's cat' or 'liquorice' or 'a tabloid journalist's soul', I would have been wrong, and lost a mark. As white as … a sheet. As flat as … a pancake. As green as … grass. Well done, Lindsay, three out of three.

What we were being taught, of course, was how to use clichés; phrases which, through over-use and over-familiarity, have lost whatever power they had to surprise us and show us the world differently.

I didn't understand this as a seven-year-old, so it's worth spelling it out now: a simile is worse than useless unless it adds something to the reader's understanding or enjoyment. And it can only do that if there is something fresh or unexpected about it.

Perhaps you've already seen the following similes which, according to one of those widely circulated emails, were taken from genuine GCSE exam answers. They made me smile. But, more to the point, they all conjured up vivid – if somewhat bizarre – pictures in my mind's eye.

> John and Mary had never met. They were like two humming-birds who had also never met.

> She walked into my office like a centipede with 98 missing legs.

She had a deep, throaty, genuine laugh, like that sound a dog makes just before it throws up.

His wife's infidelity came as a rude shock, like a surcharge at a formerly surcharge-free cashpoint.

I love that last one especially. The comparison between the shock of being charged an unexpected £1.50 by an avaricious bank and a man discovering that his wife is shagging her personal trainer is so absurd, yet strangely telling, that I can't stop laughing.

But not like a drain.

solutions

Here's proof that a single word can be a CLICHÉ.

A long time ago – in the 80s, I suspect – somebody, somewhere had a moment of insight. What this brilliantly original thinker realised was that, in many cases, people don't actually want to buy a specific product or service; what they want is a solution to a problem[6].

For example, nobody wants accountancy software; but they do want (and urgently need) a solution to the problem of how to unscramble their business finances.

---

[6]Theodore Levitt, a marketing guru of an earlier generation, expressed this insight far more elegantly: 'What people want isn't a quarter inch drill; it's a quarter inch hole'.

And so the solutions boom began.

Perhaps for a year or two, it seemed fresh. But soon, absolutely everybody was at it. Need a new secretary? Get on the phone to the recruitment solutions experts. Blocked loo? Call drainage solutions on this number. Negative energy in your bedroom? Lucky you know that Feng Shui solutions outfit.

Any day now, I'm expecting my friend Dave to rebrand himself as a supplier of 'dairy beverage solutions'.

spelling

Your computer spell-check can prevent you from spelling words incorrectly. But the importune thin to dismember is that it won't cheque weather they are the rite worms.

story

Bad writers look at a pile of facts, figures, opinions and assorted information and say, 'What order shall I put these in?'

Good writers say, 'What's the story?'

style

Hmm, this is going to be tricky. No book about how to be a better writer can ignore it; but style is slippery, amorphous stuff. We all know roughly what we mean by it, but to define it, to pin it down … well, that's a great deal harder.

And now I come to think about it, I find that I have just two simple (some might say simplistic) suggestions relating to the style you should adopt when writing persuasively:

- Forget about style, remember the reader.
- Be yourself.

Let's take them one at a time. When I write, I never consciously think about style. (Pause for sarcastic gibes to the effect that maybe I should give it a try.) What I do think about – as you'll know, unless you've just parachuted in – is my reader.

Who is this person whose thoughts, feelings or actions I want to influence? Is she knowledgeable about the subject? Sceptical, or even hostile? Does she have entrenched views? Is she reading because she needs to or because she wants to? Is she standing on a railway platform? Is she six years old?

Everything I know – or deduce or guess to be true – about my reader will help me shape the content of the story I'm going to tell; where to begin; what to include and what to leave out.

Equally, my understanding of the reader will very largely dictate the way I write. (No need to be over-explicit with a knowledgeable reader; not a good idea to be over-familiar with a sceptic; try to entertain her if she's waiting for a train; steer clear of words with more than two syllables if she's six; and so on.)

It isn't rocket science. It's what we all do every day, in conversation; automatically adjusting the way we talk – our vocabulary, the rhythm of our speech, the directness or allusiveness of what we say; our assumptions about what is or isn't funny; even, sometimes, our accent – depending on the person we're speaking to.

So, to a very large extent, style is the politeness of persuasive writers; a recognition that the reader's interests should always come first.

But that doesn't mean that a good persuasive writer should be some kind of verbal shape-shifter; an infinitely adaptable voice without any true identity. That certainly isn't true of the very best writers in the world of professional persuasion. Whatever they are writing about, and whoever the reader may be, they have a voice that is distinctive and highly recognisable.

If we return to the comparison with everyday conversation, we can see that there isn't, in fact, any contradiction here. When you talk to your granny you don't talk the same as you would in a job interview, or if you bumped into your mate in the street. But, unless you suffer from some kind of personality disorder, it's still you talking; you remain true to yourself.

'Style is the man,' said some now-forgotten French aristocrat, a couple of centuries ago. And I agree, with the obvious proviso that, in the 21st century, it's just as likely to be the woman.

So, there we are. That's all I have to say on style. Hope it helps.

T

testimonial

> 'In my view, Lindsay Camp is unquestionably the finest freelance writer I have had the privilege to meet – and also, I may add, a very fine human being. I would unhesitatingly recommend him to anyone.'
>
> Mrs P A Camp

Thanks, Mum – for proving my point, which is that, while third party testimonials can be very effective, they need to be used with some caution. Because, just like any other component of persuasive writing, they will rarely be taken entirely at face value.

Who is this person, the reader may ask herself, whose views are supposed to influence me? Or, more cynically, what's in it for the person making this glowing recommendation? (And don't think she won't ask this even if it's Richard Branson or the Pope.)

Go ahead, use appropriate testimonials in your persuasive writing. But don't imagine that the fact a third party is prepared to endorse your point of view will ever clinch the argument.

Thesaurus

Be chary using a Lexicon to aid you scribble. It can be nifty when you're wedged for a word; but habitually, the not compulsory synonyms have a poles apart meaning, or don't really construct sagacity in the milieu[7].

And anyway, what's wrong with the word you thought of in the first place? You're not searching for a different word just to impress your reader with the breadth of your vocabulary, are you?

trust

If, as a persuasive writer, you lose your reader's trust, you've lost everything.

[7]Be careful using a Thesaurus to help you write. It can be useful when you're stuck for a word; but often, the suggested synonyms have a different meaning, or don't really make sense in the context.

U

unique

Is it? Really? In that case, don't insult your reader's INTELLIGENCE by claiming that it is.

UPPER CASE

IT'S OFTEN SAID THAT ANY PIECE OF WRITING WHICH APPEARS ENTIRELY IN UPPER CASE, ESPECIALLY IF IT'S QUITE LONG AND THE FONT IS A LARGE SIZE, CAN BE HARD TO READ, AND I'M INCLINED TO AGREE, AREN'T YOU?

utilise

Just as your mum puts on a funny voice when she answers
the phone, so a lot of people have a tendency to write in a
completely different 'voice' from the one they speak in.
In particular, they utilise longer words than normal, thinking
they sound more impressive. They don't. They just make
readers feel that someone is trying to impress them; not the
same thing at all.

✗	✔
demonstrate	show
endeavour	try
select	choose
assist	help
request	ask
inform	tell
require	need
consume	eat
additional	extra
superior	better
peruse	read
approximately	about
sufficient	enough
in excess of	more than
adjacent to	next to
in the vicinity of	near
prior to	before
refrain from	don't
funds[8]	money
etc etc etc	etc

[8] Interestingly, a word with fewer syllables can sometimes be bigger and
more self-important than the everyday word it replaces.

V

verbing

Normally, I try to give reasoned arguments to support my beliefs about good and bad uses of language. But, on this occasion, I can't be bothered. I just want to state quite unequivocally that verbing – taking innocent nouns and forcing them to behave as if they were verbs – is morally repugnant; an evil practice that must, at all costs, be stamped out.

'How will this initiative impact you?' What's wrong with, 'How will it affect you?'

'We have been tasked by the client with … ' So that would be, 'The client has asked us to … '

And here's one I'm really hating in the run-up to the Olympics: 'I'm definitely hoping to medal in Athens … '

Just don't do it, OK?

vocabulary

Yes, of course it's true that good writers have big ones. (They're also unusually fond of innuendo.) But no, that isn't what makes them good writers.

W

weasel words

You know the kind of thing I mean: 'With XYZ Slim-o-Shakes, used as part of a calorie-controlled diet, you could lose up to 25lbs in under two weeks.'

It doesn't fool anyone. Don't do it.

wit

What is wit? In my book, it's all about not saying exactly what you mean. Why would a persuasive writer – who presumably wants to be understood – do such a thing? The short answer is, to involve and 'reward' the reader.

Take IRONY, for example. By writing the opposite of what I really mean, I'm not aiming to confuse you. I'm aiming to give you the opportunity to supply my true meaning; and by enlisting your participation in this way, I'm hoping that I may perhaps increase both your understanding and enjoyment of what you are reading.

Other forms of written wit – similes and metaphors, 'negatives', understatement, even puns – work in slightly different ways. But, in every case, they leave the reader a bit of work to do; conjuring up an image, making a connection, drawing a conclusion.

Think of wit as verbal Viagra: a little something that can spice up the relationship between reader and writer.

X

XXXX

Love letters, of course: the only form of persuasive writing that does have a divine right to be read. (Assuming, of course, that the reader feels roughly the same way about the writer.)

Y

you

The single most important word in persuasive writing. If you ever find that you have written more than a couple of sentences without using it, then you probably should reconsider the first couple of sentences you have written – bearing in mind how you would feel if you were the reader and the writer didn't seem to be aware that you existed.

yourself

The hardest subject to write persuasively about.

Z

ZZZZZzzzzz

Remember what I said about BEING BORING? I thought I might conclude this little jaunt through the alphabet with an example which caught my eye in today's paper. One of our largest chemical companies had spent a hefty chunk of its shareholders' money producing a large full-colour ad, with the headline:

Strategic partnerships bring new perspectives and innovative solutions.

Um ... sorry, what was that you said? I'm afraid I must have dozed off.

Section Three

Persuasive words at work

Chapter 5
How a persuasive writer writes

An attempt to get inside the head of a professional persuasive writer, and examine some of the thought processes taking place there; the three phases of a typical persuasive writing project; and some thoughts on how the left and right sides of the brain divide the responsibilities between them, like job-sharers. Well, a little bit like that.

I've always loved those articles in Sunday supplements in which well-known authors describe how they produce their international best-sellers. (I've noticed, incidentally, that it nearly always seems to involve using a fountain pen, and working in a garden shed, which is slightly depressing for me, since I possess neither.) I suppose the enjoyment is partly to do with simple curiosity about the lives of the richly gifted and famous; but another factor, I think, is that I like to be reminded that writing – even the most elevated and artistic kind – is a job of work, requiring tools, a place of business and even a certain amount of physical effort, just like being a dentist or repairing vacuum cleaners.

So I was planning to attempt something in a similar vein. On reflection, though, I think that, until I've written at least one international best-seller, it would probably be unwise to expect anyone to have the faintest interest in what I wear when I'm writing, how many coffee breaks I allow myself, or the identity of my favourite typeface.

But, while the physical shape of my working life may not be of any pressing concern to you, I think it might be useful if I tried to give an account of some of the mental processes involved in what I do. And, to that end, I'm going to talk in some detail about what goes on inside this persuasive writer's head, during the three stages of a typical job: before I start to write; the writing itself; and after I've written.

Incidentally, it's worth stressing that I'm not suggesting the way I go about the business of writing is, in any sense, the right or only way. It's just my way. I hope you may pick up a few ideas that will be useful to you, but if you have a completely different approach that works for you, don't even think about changing it.

Stage 1: before writing

Nearly every job I do begins with a written brief. And if, as somebody or other once said, the secret of good persuasive writing is to 'Remember the Reader and the Result', the purpose of this document is to jog my memory.

Sadly, most of the briefs I receive aren't very good. That's to say, they usually contain a lot of information, but very little in the way of insight or incisiveness. So the first thing I need to do, in the vast majority of cases, is to ask the person responsible for briefing me a lot of questions.

1 Interrogating the brief (or the 'yes, but' process)

I talked at great length in the first part of the book about the vital importance of being clear about the result that a piece of writing is intended to achieve, and of understanding the reader. So I'll try not to labour this here. But I do want to give you an idea of what a persuasive writer should be looking for in a brief. In 99 cases out of 100, I ask slight variants of four main questions:

Yes, but what's the single most important objective?

Many briefs are far from clear about this. Often, they present a longish shopping list of goals that the client would like to achieve:

- Increase sales by 50%
- Continue to build brand awareness among target audience
- Demonstrate commitment to retail partners
- Boost morale of head office staff
- Encourage repeat purchase among existing customers

- Encourage lapsed users to reconsider purchase
- End world hunger and pave way to peace in Middle East

… and so on. Leaving aside which of these objectives any single piece of communication could realistically be expected to achieve, my main concern is always to narrow the list down. Before I start work, I want to agree on one specific objective that takes priority over all the others.

Yes, but what is the reader like?

Most briefs tell me who will be reading my work. But often, they provide only the sketchiest biographical details: 'ABC1 males, aged 35–54', for example. Even when they describe who the reader is more fully – 'HR managers working for FTSE-100 companies, typically responsible for 2,000+ employees; evenly split male/female' – I'm still not satisfied. I want to know what the reader is like. I want the brief to give me some insight into what kind of person I'm talking to; what matters to them, what their attitudes are likely to be; what will excite or bore them.

Yes, but what's different or better about what we're selling?

Most briefs describe the product or service being sold in a fair amount of detail. But, surprisingly often, they fail to address the above question. And when they do, they tend to answer it from the client's point of view, rather than the reader's ('the product features a new all-aluminium spring mechanism precision-engineered to tolerances of 0.1 microns'). If I don't have a good reason why the reader should prefer and choose whatever it is we're selling, how am I going to write anything remotely persuasive?

Yes, but why should the reader believe that?

OK, so we have a compelling claim to make: say, our product or service can save the reader hundreds of pounds a month. But is it believable? How, exactly, does the saving accrue? If I were the reader, being offered this remarkable money-saving opportunity, would it sound credible to me?

A long time ago, a famous advertising man gave the following advice to copywriters: 'The consumer isn't a moron. She is your wife.' Today, this sounds gob-smackingly patronising, but the underlying sentiment remains sound. I would want to go further, though. When you write persuasively, I would advise you to test the credibility of what you are claiming not just against what your wife, husband or significant other would be willing to believe, but also against what you yourself would be willing to believe.

I realise that when you write persuasively, you're probably not presented with a written brief. So the last couple of pages may not seem relevant to you. But I think they are. For one thing, I would warmly recommend that next time you have a difficult piece of writing to do, you should try producing a brief for yourself. To help you, I've included a typical briefing form of the kind used in the advertising and design industry in the PS section at the back of this book. Completed with intelligence and insight, it's a remarkably powerful tool for analysing what the client (in this case, you) has to say and how that might be both relevant and motivating to the reader. It doesn't guarantee that the end result will be a powerful piece of communication, but it massively increases the likelihood.

But, even if you don't feel that writing yourself a brief would be helpful, the interrogation process I've described is indispensable. Every assumption you start out with about what you are going to write, why your reader will find it interesting, and how the words you use will help you achieve the result you want can, and probably should be questioned.

2 Background reading/pre-thinking

I remember that the very first copywriting manual I read, many years ago, told me that I should always have the client's product on my desk when I was writing. Not easy if the client manufactures jet engines or advises on corporate finance deals, but basically sound advice, nevertheless. It's perfectly true that there is no substitute for really thorough first-hand knowledge of what you are writing about.

But I have to admit that, when I write, my knowledge of the subject is often rather less encyclopaedic than I would like. It's simply a matter of time. When a job is needed yesterday if not sooner, as is often the case, it just isn't possible to visit the factory, or interview the finance director, or mystery-shop the store. It's a shame, but there it is.

Most of my familiarisation with what I'm writing about, therefore, is done by reading – product literature, websites, marketing strategies, research reports, whatever. Meanwhile, I'm doing something that may sound slightly strange: I'm consciously not thinking about the job. That's to say, at this stage, I make a point of not attempting to solve the communications problem posed by the brief; and certainly not thinking about what I'm going to write. If I had to explain this (and I suppose I must), I'd say that I think it's a mistake to let the conscious mind start baking the cake before the subconscious has assembled and sorted the ingredients. And, less poetically, I've coined a phrase for this zen-like mental inactivity that comes before the big intellectual push: pre-thinking. I rather like it. ('Are you sure you've really pre-thought this through?')

3 What's the idea?

Now the most difficult part of any job can't be postponed any longer. I need an idea.

I'm using that word in a rather specialised sense, so let me explain what I mean. In this context, an idea is the component which (I hope) will make whatever I'm writing engaging to my reader. What this component actually consists of can vary enormously from one job to another, but the function it performs is always the same: to make a connection with the reader which makes her feel that the story I have to tell is worth the time it will take her to hear it.

It follows, then, that the stronger the story, the less hard my idea will have to work to seize and hold my reader's attention. And, conversely, when I'm arguing a weaker case, I'm going to need a more compelling idea. What does that mean in practice? To demonstrate, let's take two fairly extreme points on a hypothetical spectrum representing degrees of difficulty in persuasive writing.

First, at the easy-peasy end, we're writing to inform Candidate A that, following her interview, XYZ Corporation is delighted to offer her the job, at a starting salary of £N,000, subject to a three-month review. We don't need to be very persuasive, do we? In fact, you may well be thinking that we don't need to be persuasive at all. But we do, since Candidate A may well have received job offers from other companies, and we want our letter to make XYZ's offer more attractive than theirs. What kind of idea will help us achieve this? A teeny weeny one, to be honest. In fact, I'd suggest that the 'idea' we're looking for in this case is nothing more than what I've said above: the little flicker of insight which revealed that Candidate A might have other irons in the fire. Our idea-ette is to write the letter in a way that reflects our understanding that she probably has a choice.

At the other end of that spectrum I mentioned, we need to produce an ad campaign for – well, what? I was going to say beer, but I've mentioned it before, and I don't want you to think I'm obsessed. So, let's say that Supermarket XYZ is about to launch its new online shopping service. Supermarket XYZ.com is basically no different from Tesco.com or Sainsburystoyou.co.uk, it's just arrived about four years later. So we're going to need a BIG idea.

Let's brainstorm it. I know ... how about a campaign starring a sassy little girl called Amy, who teaches her dumb, technophobic dad how to find his way around the virtual store, and click his mouse when he finds what he needs? No? Then here's another idea: we could base the campaign on the benefit of internet shopping – i.e. the amount of time it can save busy people. I'm seeing a series of posters, each showing a different online shopper doing something vaguely eccentric or picturesque. Say, just as a starter for 10, a bloke building a cathedral from matchsticks or a woman meditating on a Scottish mountainside. And, along the bottom, next to the Supermarket XYZ.com logo, a discreet line of type reading: 'What will you do with the time you save?'

Still not happy? Well, you come up with a better idea, then. And while you're thinking, I'll move on to make the point which all this has been building up to. Which is that, in my view, the success of every piece of persuasive communication depends on an idea of some kind. Usually, in your writing, you won't need a big one, like – well, like the one I'm waiting to hear for Supermarket XYZ.com. But, if you want to connect with your reader, you will, invariably, need a brief flicker of insight about how what you have to say intersects with what she might be interested to hear; a tiny lateral leap – more of a sideways shuffle – that will enable you to shape your story in a way that makes it fresh and compelling.

4 Structure and content: a brief outline

With an idea in mind, I'll soon be ready to start writing. But, if the finished piece will be more than a couple of pages long, there's one more preliminary stage: producing an outline/synopsis. At its simplest, this might consist of half a dozen bullet points on the back of an envelope. But, more often, I'll produce a fairly detailed document which includes suggested headings for each section; a description of the content that will be covered under each of these; and some indication of the proposed style.

There are two reasons for doing this. The first is to demonstrate to the client how the idea will actually work. Let's say, for example, that I have proposed to a client in the catering business that they should produce a corporate brochure that takes the form of a recipe book. Understandably, my client may not immediately see how this idea will be able to accommodate the fact that his company has recently introduced a revolutionary new cook-chill system, or won an Investors in People award. So, at this stage, I'll need to come up with, say, 10 recipes each of which enables me to make a slightly different competitive claim on behalf of XYZ Catering.

The second reason for writing an outline – which, unlike the first, will certainly be relevant to you – is to get my own thinking straight. The ideas stage of a persuasive writing project is 'creative' in character. It's all about looking for an unexpected insight or a rarely made connection; and, to that end, it involves allowing the mind to roam freely, to flit from one image or association to the next, to wander at will. But now it's time to impose a little discipline. The logical left side of the brain takes charge, and the idea is subjected to a ruthless interrogation. How does it work, precisely? How, within the constraints of the idea, should the main argument be structured? How much supporting evidence will be needed to clinch the argument? And should the bit about the client's new quality control process come before or after the section about his international distribution network? (Or, of course, should it be left out on the grounds that, while the client may want to talk about it, the reader won't find it interesting?)

Writing an outline or synopsis enables me to organise my material, marshal the arguments and provide myself with a blueprint for the finished piece of writing; a set of plans which I will be able to refer back to when I'm locked in ferocious single combat with the English language – attempting to wrestle an intransigent metaphor to the ground, maybe – during the next phase of the process; the actual writing bit.

Stage 2: writing

So, I've interrogated the brief; I've done my reading, research and pre-thinking; I've had a big, medium-sized or minuscule idea, as appropriate to the persuasive task in hand; I've written an outline, which has enabled me to determine the structure and content of the finished piece ... now all I have to do is write the damn thing.

Should be a piece of cake, shouldn't it? Well, up to a point. Certainly, it's true that I usually do find writing quite a bit less gruelling than the preliminaries that precede it. Partly, of course, that's because those preliminaries are the spadework; the back-breaking toil that has to take place before the Fancy Dan bricklayer arrives, and the walls rapidly start to take shape. And partly, I suppose, it's because stringing words and sentences together is something that, most of the time at least, comes fairly naturally to me. (I believe anyone can learn to be a better writer; but I suspect that real verbal fluency is, if not inborn, acquired in the early years of life.)

In any case, I'm rarely stuck for words. But describing the mental process which produces them ... well, er ... um, where do I start?

Unlike Professor Hawking, and despite the fact that my subject is a lot less complicated than his, I can't offer you a Single Unified Theory. But, if we begin at the beginning, I think I can provide a few insights into how the rather wonderful metamorphosis of thought into words takes place. And what to do when it won't.

1 How's this for openers?

I said quite a bit in Section Two about the critical importance of the opening lines of any piece of persuasive writing. So I'll restrict myself here to a couple of brief follow-up points.

The first is that, when faced by a blank screen and a blinking cursor, I don't think of a compelling opening line, I *feel* for one. I know roughly what I want to say, and where the argument is going to lead me; but it's very rarely logic that dictates what those first few words should be. I think about who the reader is, how and where she's likely to be reading, and how I want her to respond. And then – sometimes soon, but often after a lengthy wait, and another cup of coffee – an opening phrase or sentence forms in my mind.

Then, the rational mind takes charge. If those are the opening words, what needs to follow immediately? Usually, in the manner of a newspaper front page lead, the job of my first paragraph or two will be to provide the reader with a potted version of the whole story; giving her, at the earliest opportunity, the chance to decide whether it's worth her while to read on. But, just occasionally, I may feel that I can afford to be less up-front; to begin the meeting without, so to speak, an agenda. In which case, the first few sentences I write will need to be so intriguing or otherwise engaging that my reader won't be able to resist the invitation to set off into the unknown with me. Once in a while, it's a risk worth taking.

2 Finding the right words

Let's try an experiment. I'm going to write a sentence, like this. Actually, no, it will have to be a longer one, because what I'm planning to do is write a sentence – like this – and, while I'm actually writing it, think very hard about how I'm doing it.

In fact, I've been doing that quite a bit lately, and I have reached a few tentative conclusions. The first is that, for me, writing is almost exactly the same as talking, only with more time. That's to say, I form phrases and sentences in my head when I'm writing in precisely the same way as I do when I'm having a conversation – but because there isn't a real live human being sitting across the table from me, looking enraptured or quizzical or bored to death, I can go back over the phrases and sentences and remodel them until I'm happy with them. In writing, then, what the French rather charmingly call 'l'esprit de l'escalier' – the thing you wished you'd said when you're going down the stairs and it's too late – comes as standard.

Let's examine the similarity between talking and writing a bit more closely. When I talk – and I suspect you are the same – I nearly always start without knowing exactly how I'm going to finish. What happens, I've observed, is that as I am talking, a word or short phrase, representing the next idea I want to express, bubbles up in my mind. The effect, I imagine, is rather similar to a TV interviewer hearing his producer's voice in his earpiece, prompting him about the next question he should ask. As I continue to talk, I start mentally constructing a bridge that will take me from what I'm saying now to the idea or phrase in question. Being articulate, I suspect, is largely a matter of how quick and skilful a bridge-builder one is.

Take away the pressure to complete the building work on time, and this is also exactly how I write – right down to the fact that I often begin a sentence without knowing how it will end. I'm not even slightly apologetic about this: almost always, I want my writing to be conversational; to sound like a friendly and knowledgeable voice, chatting away inside your head.

Having said that, there are times when, in order to make what I have to say more engaging, I deliberately write a sentence more complex in structure than anything I'd usually say in conversation. Scanning the last couple of pages, I find this example:

> Unlike Professor Hawking, and despite the fact that my subject is a lot less complicated than his, I can't offer you a Single Unified Theory.

Let me try to tell you exactly how I wrote that sentence. I thought, rationally, that I wanted to make it clear that my remarks on the mental processes involved in writing were precisely that – a few fairly random remarks, not a coherent, scientifically tested theory. The phrase 'Single Unified Theory' sprang to mind, bringing with it a mental picture of the world's best-known wheelchair-user. So now the sentence started to take shape. Instead of following ordinary conversational word order ('I want to make it clear that what I'm about to say isn't intended to be a coherent, scientifically tested theory ... '), I put Professor Hawking first, to make the sentence more interesting for the reader. And then, after I'd written this ...

Unlike Professor Hawking, I can't offer you a Single Unified Theory.

... I decided, rather riskily, to add this:

... and despite the fact that my subject is a lot less complicated than his ...

Why? Because I thought that it would make the sentence even more interesting and enjoyable; by first intriguing the reader ('what the hell has Stephen Hawking got to do with persuasive writing?'), then deliberately postponing the moment of realisation; and finally delivering the pay-off.

I like that sentence; I think it works. But, whether or not you agree, my point is that, however much writing may resemble talking, there are also important differences; things I can do on the page or screen that I'd never try face to face. Because, just as I have more time to find the right words when I'm writing, so my reader has a little more leisure to unravel my meaning.

And there's one other crucial way that, for me, talking and writing are similar. Er, I talk when I write. I can't help it. As I'm sitting here tapping away at the keys, I'm muttering every single word to myself. True, it would make me a nightmare to share an office with; but nevertheless, I'd warmly recommend this slightly disturbing practice. Speaking the words as I'm writing them is an indispensable way of testing them: I hear a weedy word or a puny phrase as soon as I utter it; and I'm immediately aware if a sentence fails to flow, or the emphasis falls in the wrong place. For me, writing in silence would be roughly to equivalent to cooking without seasoning (or maybe swearing) for Gordon Ramsay.

3 Unleashing the subconscious

I've already touched on this, I know, but I want to expand a bit on the role played by the non-rational mind in making writing come alive.

Similes are a particularly good illustration of what I'm talking about. On a recent holiday in the south of France, I was walking along a country lane, lined with large houses set back from the road. As I came level with each house, a huge ferocious-sounding dog would race out from inside and bark furiously at me – until it was perfectly satisfied that I was continuing on my way, and meant its owners no harm. Then, as I came to the next house, another dog would emerge and give a repeat performance; and so on at each house, along the lane.

An image sprang into my mind. The dogs were like air traffic controllers – each shepherding me through its own portion of 'airspace', before handing me on to the next.

This simile made me smile. But the reason I mention it is because I'd like you to consider where such images come from. Absolutely nowhere. That's to say, they emerge, unbidden, from the subconscious. No mental effort or rational thought process is involved. The mind takes one piece of information and cross-references it with another; forming a connection that allows a current to flow through the sentence, resulting – however briefly – in a flash of illumination.

True, good writers must be logical thinkers, otherwise coherence and compelling argument go out of the window. But unless we can also learn to let our creative subconscious off the leash, our writing will lack freshness and colour. I do that, usually, by staring blankly into space, and deliberately emptying my head of conscious thought, like … a vicar chucking the Rotary Club out of the church hall, to make space for a playgroup full of hyperactive toddlers.

While we're on the subject of allowing instinct and intuition to play their part, it's also worth recording that I quite often fold up the plans, shove them in my back pocket, and redesign the building as I'm actually constructing it. It wouldn't work with real bricks and mortar; but, as a creator of verbal edifices, I find that thought processes have a tendency to evolve as I put them into words. Sometimes one idea, when expressed, clearly leads on to another – despite the fact that I wasn't planning to cover them in that order. Or a single word or phrase suggests a connection with another part of my material which I hadn't previously spotted. And 19 times out of 20, I'll follow where an idea or instinct leads.

4 Editing and appearances

Of course, I edit as I write. For less experienced writers, I think there's a good case for just splurging it all down as fast as possible, from beginning to end, and then going back to cut and shape it afterwards. But, partly for practical reasons, I prefer to do that in real time.

The practical reasons are to do with deadlines. Nearly always, I'm writing against the clock, so I want to ensure that when I get to the end of a piece of writing, it's very nearly finished: just a quick read through; a couple of final tweaks; and then I can hit 'send'. Of course, it doesn't always work out like this. But usually, when I get to the end of a paragraph or the bottom of a page, I don't continue until I'm 95% happy with what I've written.

Editing, incidentally, isn't about trying to make what you've written shorter. That may be the effect; but the aim, as ever, is to make the words on the page or screen more engaging to the reader. This means continually asking the following questions:

1 'Will my reader find what I've just written interesting or useful or enjoyable?'
2 'What could I do to make it more interesting/useful/ enjoyable for my reader?'

If the answer to question 1 is no, out it goes. But, depending on my answer to question 2, I may actually add rather than subtract something (I'm thinking, for example, of my Professor Hawking sentence). Or I may exchange one word for a more accurate one. Or get rid of a weary phrase and replace it with something perkier. Or delete a sentence that doesn't make sense. Or change the order in which a sentence is constructed. Or simplify the punctuation.

And at this stage, while I'm in full flow, I'm not just thinking about the sound and meaning of the words I'm writing. I'm also concerned with how they look.

As a persuasive writer, it's my job to do everything I can to make my work as appealing as possible to the reader. (You remember, the one who has better things to do.) And, like it or not, that includes giving careful thought to how it will appear on the page or screen. I'm as irritated as anyone by ads in which every sentence, however short, forms a new paragraph. But I would concede that large uninterrupted areas of dense typography can look quite daunting to an uncommitted reader. So I never let my paragraphs reach Dickensian lengths.

I often chuck in sub-headings, too

… just to break it up a bit, and make it easier on the eye. And, as I mentioned earlier:

- I'm
- not
- completely
- averse
- to
- bullet
- points
- if used appropriately

Or little boxes with key points inside them – preferably in bold type.

Of course, I'd like my reader to give me her undivided attention. But I know that she may well be skimming through what I've written – lunchtime sandwich in one hand, phone clamped to ear – trying to get the gist of it, in under two minutes. If there's anything I can do to help, I will.

5 Writer's block: what happens when the words won't come?

I seem to remember making some rather smug remarks a few pages back about how easy I find it to crank out metre after metre of flowing prose. Um, not always the case. Sometimes, I sweat over every word And sometimes … well, sometimes it just won't happen. I sit, fingers poised over keyboard, mind a perfect blank.

Actually, I'm surprised this doesn't happen more often. Because, when you think about it, writing is a pretty scary business. Consider, for example, this simple sentence:

I love tennis.

Perfectly clear, isn't it? Except that it may give the impression that what I love is watching tennis on TV. So I should probably write:

I love playing tennis.

Yes, that's better. Hmm, but maybe it feels a bit weak …

I absolutely love playing tennis.

Nah. Don't like absolutely – something rather forced about it. Perhaps this might be better:

I don't like tennis; I love it.

Yes, that's great. No, hang on, just realised I've nicked it from that really rubbish song that 10cc did back in the 70s – you remember, 'I don't like reggae, I love it' … So that's no good. Ha! What about this …

For the last 10 years, I've been conducting a passionate love affair. With tennis.

Or:

For me, tennis isn't just a game, it's …

... well, I guess I've made the point, which is that the scary thing about writing is that there is way too much choice. Even the most banal sentiment can be expressed in a virtually unlimited number of different ways. To be a writer means to be constantly facing decisions; attempting to find precisely the right words, from literally millions of possible combinations.

How do writers learn to overcome this fear and the paralysis it induces? I'm not sure. Answering for myself, I can only say that I'm fortified by the knowledge that there are no right answers. Nobody in the world knows better than me what I want to say; and if I'm happy that the words I've chosen to express it will connect with my reader, nobody can tell me that I'm wrong.

I'm afraid that last paragraph may sound glib ('just do what feels right, and take no notice of what anyone else says'). But, for me, it contains quite an important truth – and one which took me an awfully long time to recognise. Until quite recently, I imagined that, whatever I was doing, there were other people, expert in that field, who knew precisely how it should be done. Very rarely the case, I've come to believe. Most of the time, in most fields, most people muddle through. Some muddle more successfully than others; and those who have muddled to reasonably good effect on a number of occasions, gradually gain confidence in their own skills and judgement. I find this thought very liberating – generally, and especially in relation to writing, where I've done more than my share of not-too-disastrous muddling.

The consolations of philosophy apart, what can I tell you about how I cope when the words refuse to flow? Easily the most effective measure is to stop trying. If consciously straining and striving to express what I need to say doesn't work, I leave it for 10 minutes, a couple of hours or overnight, depending how much time I've got. This, of course, is to allow the subconscious to go to work. I remember hearing that if you read the clues of a cross-word on Monday, then forget all about them, you'll be able to solve them in seconds if you re-read them on Friday. I've never tried it with a crossword; but I can vouch for the effectiveness of this technique when applied to persuasive writing projects.

What if I'm working to a tight deadline, and I really don't have even 10 minutes to spare? Then I remind myself that when a writer runs into difficulties, it's very rarely words that are the real problem. Almost always, confused or over-complicated thinking is to blame.

To give you an idea how this helps me in practice, let's switch, briefly, to a different language. I'm not very good at French. But I'm still a bit better than either of my school-age kids, so they quite often ask me to help with their homework. 'Hey Dad,' they say, 'What's the French for: "System of a Down are way cool, unlike those sad tossers Limp Bizkit who suck ass big style"?'

Needless to say, I don't have a clue. So what I tell them is this: if you don't know the right way to say what you want to say, don't say it. Say something else instead. Something you do know how to say. (In this case, I could just about manage 'System of a Down are my favourite group, but I don't like Limp Bizkit at all.')

And actually, I find the same applies when the language is English. If something I want to say just won't come out right, it may be that I just don't have the words to capture that particular thought process. So I look at it from a different angle. Turn it back to front. Simplify it. True, I may lose something by doing this: but better a slightly less complex idea clearly expressed than a confused reader. N'est-ce pas?

Still not practical enough for you? Then here's what I do when I'm really, really stuck: I ask myself, what it would be in one shortish sentence? If I only had, say 12 to 15 words, to convey what's in my head to my reader, what would they be?

6 Finishing off and polishing up

Unlike openings, I don't have a lot to say about endings. I don't share the belief commonly held by advertising copywriters that it's essential to finish any piece of persuasive writing with some agonisingly contrived play on words. I do think it's a good idea to remind your reader of your most persuasive arguments. And, usually, I'm in favour of a 'call to action' – a polite suggestion to your reader that she might like to do whatever it is you would like her to do next.

But, those considerations apart, my main approach to finishing any piece of writing is simply to stop when I run out of things to say. I suppose I do also try to ensure that my concluding couple of sentences sound ... well, conclusive. Leaving the audience in mid-air may work well in Eastern European arthouse movies, but readers of persuasive writing, I firmly believe, want closure; a satisfying sense that an act of communication has taken place, and is now finished.

> One way of achieving this effect, I find, is to end with a sentence rather longer than those that have gone before, and perhaps a little more complex in construction, creating a sense that together – reader and writer – we're putting on the brakes, approaching our destination, preparing for the moment when we go our separate ways.

It's all about rhythm; and sometimes, it works even better if I add a couple of extra beats:

> One way of achieving this effect, I find, is to end with a sentence rather longer than those that have gone before, and perhaps a little more complex in construction, creating a sense that together – reader and writer – we're putting on the brakes, approaching our destination, preparing for the moment when we go our separate ways. That moment is now.

Anyway, I've finished. And if, as is often the case, I'm pressed for time, I'll only spend a matter of minutes now polishing the finished item before sending it to the client. How do I spend those minutes? First, I'll run a spell-check – not because I need help with spelling (I'm sorry, we all have our little vanities and, since I gave up plaiting my moustache, spelling is mine), but because it's a quick way to pick up any typos or or repeated words. Next, I'll do a very quick read through, invariably muttering under my breath as I read, which allows me to hear anything nasty, like a clumsy repetition. Then, if I still have seconds to spare, I may make a few very minor cuts and changes – just losing a word here, and getting rid of a set of brackets here. (I've always had a tendency to over-use brackets, but I do try to fight it.)

Finally, if it's more than a single sheet – and it usually is – I add page numbers. Then it's ready to go.

When the deadline isn't so tight, I always leave what I've written and return to it later, preferably the next day. Basically, the process is the same; but, under less pressure, I can afford to be more perfectionist. And I may well reconstruct a sentence, or shift a paragraph, in order to make fairly marginal improvements to the sense or sound or flow of the piece.

In particular, I'm more likely to make cuts. Because, with time on my side, I'm much better able to do what every persuasive writer should always do: look at what I've written through my reader's eyes. And doing that may very well enable me to detect material that fails to pass the 3 Rs test: bearing in mind who the reader is, does what I've written make the result I want more or less likely? Speaking from my own experience, I don't think Blaise Pascal was trying to be funny when he wrote that much quoted line:

> I've made this letter longer than usual only because I didn't have time to make it shorter.

Stage 3: after writing

After I despatch the finished job, what usually happens is this. About half an hour later, the phone rings. It's the client – full of warm thanks to me for getting it done so quickly, and even warmer praise for the wit and incisiveness that oozes from my writing. Would I like to submit my invoice by email straight away, so that it can be paid immediately? I would; and next morning, there's the cheque on my doormat. And when the doorbell rings a little later, I take delivery of a case of vintage Champagne, accompanied by a note from the client, saying …

I'm sorry, I was hallucinating for a moment there; I've been under rather a lot of stress lately. What, in reality, usually happens after I hit send is that there is a longish silence.

(*Time passes. Days, weeks, months, decades. Empires rise and fall.*)

Sometimes a very long one. Then, eventually, I get feedback. And I'd like to say just a couple of words here about how I respond to it.

Very badly. Well, I'm half-joking. Because if I was really thin-skinned about the constructive and not-so-constructive comments I receive from clients, I wouldn't have been able to survive as a professional writer for several thousand years. Having said that, it's never easy.

I do think, though, that I've improved a bit in this respect, over the years; and it occurs to me that the approach I've slowly and painfully evolved might be labelled the 3 Ps of responding to feedback:

1 **Don't panic**. Often, the first feedback I receive is scarily negative (quite brave of me to admit that, actually). The impression I'm given is that the job is a disaster; everything is wrong, the piece will have to be rewritten from scratch. Nearly always, it turns out to be a lot less bad than that. In fact, quite frequently it turns out that it's just a handful of individual words or phrases that are causing the client concern; the kind of problems I can fix in five or 10 minutes. So the first step is not to over-react; to remember that people often focus on the doorknobs rather than considering the architecture of the entire building.

2 **Don't take it personally**. This is a lot harder. Because, however professional a writer may be, what he writes is highly personal. There's no getting away from it: when

I write, I'm pouring out the contents of my brain on to paper. And if you look at that paper, and scrawl 'NO!' across it in red ink – or 'Clumsy!' or 'This sentence is meaningless' or even '???' – well, I'm sorry if it makes me sound like a wimp, but that is going to hurt.

3 **Don't get pissed off**. Sometimes the feedback I get is not just insensitively expressed but, frankly, dumb. I'm tempted to catalogue some of the more foolish requests and comments I've received. But that way embittered whingeing lies. So, instead, I'll mention just one generic example: the fairly common request to cut the length of what I've written ... while, at the same time, adding a couple of sentences about this, and a paragraph or two about that. Getting cross, I've learned, doesn't help. Sometimes, in such situations, it's possible to reason with people; sometimes he who pays the writer insists on calling the tune, however verbally discordant it may turn out to be.

Dammit, I've just thought of a fourth P:

4 **Be positive**. Rather grudgingly, I have to admit that there are occasions when feedback actually helps. If I've implied above that this writer always knows best, and that anyone reacting less than favourably to every word he writes is an illiterate and muddy-minded cretin, then I really should acknowledge that isn't the case. As you've heard, I usually work quickly. Mistakes do get occasionally made. The odd poorly constructed sentence does slip through. And sometimes I make

bigger mistakes – misplacing the emphasis, leaving out an important supporting argument, or misunderstanding how the reader may benefit from a particular feature. On such occasions, listening to feedback and responding positively will result in a better finished piece of writing. Which is, of course, all that really matters.

How to write: left, right, left, right, left, right ...

I knew before I started this book that good persuasive writing demands high-level input from both sides of the brain: the logical, order-imposing left and the rapscallion, ideas-generating right. But, as I've applied my mind to the subject, I feel I've arrived at a much clearer understanding of how the two hemispheres actually work together.

Think of it like job-sharing. Mr Left arrives at work early, and spends the morning sorting things out, putting them in order, making sure that everything makes sense. Just before lunch, Ms Right turns up and takes over. She stares into space, day-dreams a little, then scribbles down a few ideas on a pad – which she leaves on the desk for Mr Left to cast a cool, rational eye over in the morning ...

Hmm, maybe I shouldn't over-extend the analogy. Because, while it does convey a sense of how the rational and intuitive parts of the mind divide the responsibility for producing good persuasive writing, it falls down in one crucial respect. In reality, the handovers between left and right can happen very rapidly indeed; in fact, almost instantaneously – as an incisive piece of thinking sparks a bright idea which is immediately checked for relevance before a further lateral leap occurs ... and so on. If it really were a job-share, Mr Left would arrive at 9.00, Ms Left would replace him at 9.01, and they'd both be fighting over the desk about seven seconds later.

Anyway, that – as far as I'm able to find the words to describe it – is how I write. If you have a quicker, easier way that produces better results, please do let me know.

Chapter 6
Persuasive words at work

How understanding the principles of good persuasive writing can make you better at your job (whatever it is); how every word a business uses when talking to its customers can influence how they feel about it; and how every word used within a business – between management and workforce, or between colleagues – can make it work better (or worse).

Here's a question which I suspect may have flitted across your consciousness more than once as you've read this far:

> How exactly is all this stuff about persuasive writing relevant to what I do at work?

In Section One, I tried to make a case for persuasive writing as a basic life-skill. But that was a long time ago now. And I'm well aware that, for even a moderately sceptical reader, it would be quite easy to dismiss my evangelical fervour as special pleading on behalf of what I do for a living. So I think it would be a good idea if I tackled that question of yours head-on.

The answer, of course, depends on what you do. If, for example, you work in an advertising agency as a copywriter, then you probably won't need to be convinced that what you've read so far has a bearing on your work. And I guess that broadly the same may apply if you work in any branch of the persuasive communications industry: marketing, design, branding, sales promotion, PR, even journalism.

But what if you're a yoga teacher or an Independent Financial Adviser or the owner of a sandwich shop? Am I seriously suggesting that understanding the principles of good persuasive writing could really make a positive difference to your daily working life?

Well yes, I am. And the most obvious reason why is that all businesses, whatever their nature or size, have at least two things in common. Customers and competitors. And all the words any business uses to communicate with its customers can either help or hinder its efforts to distinguish itself from its competitors.

Come on, let's go for a brief stroll around my neighbourhood, and I'll show you what I mean ...

How every word the customer sees counts

First stop, the corner shop. I've been having a little trouble tying my shoelaces lately, so desperate measures are called for. I'm looking for a yoga class. But, being a bluff, no-nonsense sort of fellow, I'm rather put off by all the accompanying Eastern philosophy; I'm after a more flexible spine, not a greater ability to resonate in harmony with the Universe. So, let's see if there's anything suitable on the corner shop noticeboard. Yes, two or three local yoga classes, actually. But only one that catches my eye:

Yoga without tree-hugging.

That sounds like exactly the kind of teacher I would be comfortable with (so far as it's possible to feel comfortable with your legs knotted round the back of your neck). Suddenly gripped by a feverish desire for self-improvement, I'm also interested to see two ads offering French conversation. The first is neat, businesslike, professional-looking; the second, handwritten on a scrappy bit of paper, contains a number of obvious spelling and grammatical mistakes. I know straight away which conversationalist I'll be calling: the second, who is clearly a native French speaker.

Numbers noted, and feeling peckish, so on to the world's best sandwich shop: Fantastic Sandwich[9] on Gloucester Road in Bristol. An enormous blackboard tempts me with every imaginable combination of sandwich fillings, many of the house specials bearing frankly ridiculous names,

[9]Mostly, I've chosen to disguise the identities of the businesses that appear in these pages. But in this case, I've made an exception. Fantastic Sandwich is fantastic. Go there. Buy a sandwich. Eat it. Experience true happiness.

for example, the Errol Flynn (a reference, I believe, to the length and girth of this sausage-filled monstrosity); the Wok-out (wok-fried peppers, you see); and the King of Tonga (no idea, actually).

It's a bit silly, certainly, and the humour is on the creaky side. But, somehow, it clearly communicates that this isn't just a sandwich shop, but a shop run by and for sandwich enthusiasts; as far from Pret a Manger as my forehand volley is from Tim Henman's.

I order my usual, but when the owner presents it to me 10 minutes later (Fantastic Sandwiches are fantastic, but they're not fast), he's mildly apologetic: 'I hope you don't mind, but I got a bit spontaneous and put in dill pickles, because the avocados aren't quite ripe.'

Spontaneous! What a perfect choice of word – conjuring up, as it does, an artist suddenly inspired, rather than the owner of a sandwich shop realising that he's run out of a key ingredient, but going ahead anyway without con-sulting the customer. I thank him profusely for his spontaneity, pay him handsomely, and carry off my sand-wich, salivating.

On the corner, by the lights, there's an Independent Financial Adviser's office. Nothing swanky, just a couple of guys in their shirtsleeves, tapping away at keyboards, waiting for a customer. I notice, though, that over the door it says 'Wealth management'. A bit off-putting maybe if I'm thinking of bunging a couple of hundred quid a month in an ISA, or wondering if I can afford a slightly bigger mortgage?

Almost home now, but I need to work up an appetite for that Fantastic Sandwich, so let's just take a left and go up past the school and back through the park. I can't decide whether I'm more amused or depressed by the way that, in today's competitive education marketplace, every school has to have a slogan. This one, displayed on a board outside the main entrance, is fairly typical:

Placing value on Courtesy, Honesty, Tolerance and Calm.

Actually, now I think about it, I find that very funny – especially that 'Calm'. I suppose you can see what they're trying to do: reassure nice middle-class parents living locally that this isn't one of those nasty rough schools, where foul-mouthed young oafs terrorise teachers and disrupt classes, preventing sensitive Sebastian and musical Miranda from fulfilling their academic potential. Yet, somehow, it achieves exactly the opposite effect. Perhaps it's because 'Placing value on' is so incredibly weedy; but, whatever the reason, we feel that the Courtesy, Honesty, Tolerance and, especially, the Calm remain things that the school can only aspire to, somewhat despairingly, rather than goals that are within its reach. In any case, I suspect that most of the parents who can afford it will respond more positively to the posh girls' school up the road, which claims to be in the business of:

Nurturing talent.

Home – and while we've been out, a local estate agent has delivered a flyer, offering me 'a FREE valuation, at a time to suit my convenience'. Since I'm not planning to move in the near future, I'm not tempted; but, when the time comes, that's one estate agent I won't be calling. How stupid do they think I am, to imply that the fact they don't charge for carrying out valuations is some kind of amazing special offer? And how considerate of them to do it at a time of my choosing, rather than just turning up on my doorstep at 3am with their electronic measuring devices, as estate agents usually do.

Perhaps you feel I'm labouring the point, but I think it deserves all the emphasis I can give it. It's not just the obvious, high-profile types of persuasive communication – expensive advertising campaigns or glossy sales literature, for example – that have an impact on how a business is seen by its customers. Every word that any individual within any business (or other organisation) uses which may be read by a customer or potential customer can have either a positive or a negative influence on what that customer thinks or feels about the business, especially in relation to its competitors. The basic principles of good persuasive writing – you remember, the 3 Rs – therefore apply universally to anything you write at work that may be seen by customers.

But what about the things you write at work which no customer will ever see? We've already touched on this earlier, so you probably won't be surprised to hear me say that, whatever your trade or profession, virtually everything you write should be seen as having a persuasive aspect to it. It may not meet our original definition of true persuasive writing (the kind whose main purpose is to influence how a reader thinks, feels or behaves); but it's hard to think of a single kind of business communication where there isn't an opportunity to leave your reader feeling more warmly towards you, more inclined to be helpful to you, more likely to return your call, more willing to give you the benefit of the doubt next time you mess up.

Persuasive writing within the workplace

Let's start with the most obvious example of what I mean. In most businesses, especially large ones, individuals and departments are, to some extent, in competition with each other. You and that geeky-looking bloke from Sales may be up against each other for promotion. Your proposal may be one of half a dozen being reviewed by the Board. Your bonus may depend on how well your team is judged to have performed against another, over the last 12 months. The success of a project may depend on your ability to convince others that it's more deserving of their support than another.

Clearly, against this background, how you argue your case counts for a great deal. The person you need to persuade may be your boss; but, in effect, he or she is your customer – someone who needs to be given compelling reasons, rational and/or emotive, for preferring whatever it is you are trying to 'sell'. Neglect the 3 Rs at your peril.

What if you are the boss? I'm glad you asked me that. Because, in my experience of the workplace, nobody needs to polish up their persuasive communication skills more urgently than you.

Using words to get the worst out of people

I may be wrong about this because I'm not a management expert, but I've always assumed that one of the most important attributes of a good boss is the ability to get the best out of people. Yet many of the bosses I've observed at close quarters don't seem to understand this. Either that, or they fail to grasp the extent to which their success as motivators depends on the words they use.

So let's spell it out. Just as every customer-facing word can have a negative or a positive impact, so can every single word written or uttered by management and read or heard by those they manage.

How not to do it? Starting again at the blindingly obvious end of the scale, there are the internal communications which betray a crass insensitivity on the part of those in charge towards the concerns of those who work for them; a total failure to ask, let alone answer, the question, 'How would I feel in that person's shoes, if somebody said that to me?'

I'd guess that a couple of million all-staff emails a day fall into this category. And I'm sure I could, with diligent research, dredge up a dozen. But why go to all that trouble when I can perfectly illustrate my point by referring to a single example of this genre of internal communication, by The Master: that scene from *The Office* in which David Brent announces to his team that he has good news and bad news for them – the bad news being that they are about to lose their jobs, the good that he has been promoted ...

Of course, what I'm talking about here is a failure on the part of individual managers to put themselves in the shoes of their readers/listeners. And, since there will always be a proportion of empathy-free oafs among any group of people, I guess this kind of counterproductive management communication will always be with us. But much more depressing – and damaging – is what we might call the institutional misuse of language that routinely takes place, almost unnoticed, in many businesses and other organisations. I mean the everyday terminology – the words and phrases used to refer to people and processes – which is adopted by those at the top and then trickles down to all levels.

Consider, for example, the kind of business-school-speak that 20 years ago, perhaps, seemed fresh and dynamic, but is now so wearisomely familiar that nobody even thinks to question it. In this language, people are described as a company's assets. The function of looking after them, formerly known as personnel, is now human resource management. The organisations they work for no longer grow or develop or even change; they are re-engineered.

What effect does this kind of language have on the people who work for an organisation? Easy. It depersonalises them. True, that familiarity I mentioned may make this effect almost subliminal, but it exists nevertheless. Time and again, day after day, this message is communicated: the organisation is a machine; you are a cog; ponder your insignificance, and tremble!

Sometimes, more brutally still, management imposes a language that doesn't just attempt to crush the life out of the workers, but mounts a head-on assault on their sense of professional self-worth. I'm thinking of the introduction of market-speak into public sector areas, like the National Health Service. Many people here are driven by a belief in public service; a desire to spend their working lives making society a little better for their fellow citizens. To expect them to start talking about customers and outputs and increased productivity and target optimisation is to pour a bucket of icy water over them, and tell them to grow up and forget all that pathetic socialist baloney.

Of course, this may be the intention. But my concern here is with the way that, in many organisations, managers apparently use language without any thought for the response it's likely to elicit. Sure, go ahead and make people feel like they don't exist as human beings, and that you hold their deepest beliefs in contempt, if that's how you think you will get the best out of them. But don't be surprised if the results aren't good.

One final grouch while we're on the subject of using words to demotivate people. I hate all the relentless positivity out there in the business world of today. You know the kind of thing I mean. Being forbidden to call problems anything but opportunities. Meetings where no one is allowed to start a sentence with 'but'. The word 'empowerment'.

My visceral loathing for this corporately enforced positive thinking may simply reflect my deeply misanthropic and pessimistic nature. But I don't think so. I'm pretty sure my objection is based on the inauthenticity of this kind of language, which seeks to deny the people within an organisation the right to express honest human emotions. If I'm a junior manager and I've just learned that my targets have been increased by 150% and my budget has been cut in half, dammit, I'm facing a problem, not an opportunity. And if you won't let me call it that, you're not helping me deal with the reality of the situation I'm in.

If you were the kind of boss I was thinking of when I started writing these last few paragraphs, I know what your response would be: 'I'm the boss, I'll use whatever kind of language I damn well please.' Or perhaps, a bit less confrontationally, 'Managing people is hard work. I don't have the time or energy to worry over every little nuance of the words I use.'

But, however you were to put it (assuming you were that kind of boss, which I'm sure you're not), I'd think you were wrong. These days, people are expected to put so much into their work; not just long hours, but a degree of commitment and even passion that, in previous generations, people reserved for their families, hobbies or political beliefs. This may or may not be a good thing, but it's the modern way. And it means, of course, that employers get a very good deal. But it absolutely can't be one-sided: if people are putting their heart and soul into their work – arriving early, leaving late, willingly putting career before virtually any other commitments – they have a right to expect that their feelings will be respected. In short, emotional labour, as it's sometimes called, must be paid for with at least a degree of empathy – or, like any other kind of labour that isn't adequately rewarded, it will probably be withdrawn.

Persuasive communication and collaborative working

Perhaps I've made the average workplace sound like a fairly cut-throat environment, where the lowly are constantly vying with each other for status or more material rewards, and those in power are only concerned with squeezing every last drop of profit-enhancing performance from their hapless human resources. (For some reason, my favourite Woody Allen joke comes to mind: 'Dog eat dog? No, it's much worse than that: dog doesn't return dog's phone calls.') But I'm aware that, for many people, work isn't like that at all; and that for many more, that's only one aspect of life in the workplace.

Quite a few people are lucky enough to do work they enjoy, with people they respect and like, in a congenial environment. And even if you wouldn't put yourself in that category, you may still feel that your success at work depends more on your ability to establish productive working relationships than to skewer adversaries on a deftly turned phrase.

If that's the case – if your working life is more about collaboration than competition – how relevant are the principles of good persuasive communication to you?

Not very, I suppose. At least, not if we are talking about persuasive communication in its purest form: using words in order to achieve a specific desired result. But I'd suggest that in any relationship, professional or otherwise, it pays to be aware of the response that the words you use are likely to elicit, and to understand how that response may influence the other person's feelings or behaviour towards you.

I hope that doesn't sound cynical. It isn't meant to. In fact, far from suggesting that you should attempt to manipulate the feelings of the people you work with, I'm suggesting that you should approach your relationships with good colleagues in virtually the same way as your closest friendships – recognising the importance of the words you use in promoting (or undermining) the openness, trust, consideration and mutual good will on which both types of relationship depend.

Let's very briefly consider what this means in practice:

- Being open with colleagues means using words to reveal and illuminate rather than to conceal or complicate. If you're using professional jargon, are you quite sure that your motives are pure? That's to say, is your aim to facilitate communication between people who share a specialist vocabulary, or to make what you are saying sound more important?

- Building trust in your working relationships is, to a large extent, about using words in a way that shows respect for your colleagues' intelligence. Does that feasibility study you've written depend for its force on weasel words and phrases, like, 'potential savings of up to 15%'? Have you obviously exaggerated in support of a case you want to make? Have you omitted a key fact that clearly needs to be taken into account? If so, you may get away with it; but, as ever, the danger is that if you don't, the damage to your relationship with your 'reader' may well be irreparable.

- Sometimes, the best way of showing consideration for the people you work with is *not* to communicate with them. Or, to be more specific, not to copy them in on that email you're about to send. In a world where everyone feels themselves to be on the point of slipping below the waves in a sea of information, the kindest thing you can do for your colleagues is ask the persuasive writer's perennial question, 'Does my reader want or need to know this now?'

- Mutual good will? So important, so easy to compromise. Any of the above methods will do the trick; but here's one that's particularly effective. Using words to distance yourself from the people you work with; switching abruptly from the first person plural – 'We've made really good progress with this project' – to the second person singular – 'Sounds like you've run into difficulties ...'

Oh dear. As so often throughout the writing of this book, I find myself wondering if what I've just spent several pages saying is so glaringly obvious that the only question to be resolved is whether wasting paper or insulting your intelligence is the worst crime I've committed here. But, as on previous occasions, I'm somewhat reassured by the evidence of my own eyes. I've seen people – intelligent, hard working, ambitious people – making all of the above mistakes, apparently unaware that the words they were using might be hindering them from establishing happy and productive working relationships.

Originally, I was planning to end this chapter with a bit of speculation about whether there might be anyone out there in the world of work who would have absolutely nothing to gain from understanding the principles of good persuasive communication. It would, of course, have been a rhetorical device, intended – by underlining how incredibly few such occupations exist – to reinforce my argument about the near-universal relevance of this book.

But then I thought it might be better to make my point by means of a specific example: by introducing you to someone whose work would appear to have little or nothing to do with persuasion, but who, when you look more closely, turns out to need a sound grasp of persuasive principles.

Have you met my wife, Anna? She's a commercial lawyer, which means she spends much of her time drafting contracts between businesses. Nothing in the least persuasive about that, you're probably thinking. And Anna would tend to agree. The most important feature of a well-drafted contract, she tells me, is a complete absence of ambiguity. Because, if there is anything that can be interpreted in a way that gives the other side a commercial advantage, it almost certainly will be.

But think, for a moment, about how Anna arrives at that watertight unambiguousness. By looking at every single word she writes from the point of view of a reader, whose agenda and thought processes she needs to understand. Just like a persuasive writer does.

And perhaps there is a case to be made (m'lud) that a good legal contract is also, to some degree, persuasive in intent. Because, when you come to think about it, any lawyer drafting a contract has one very clear objective: to find a form of words that promotes her client's interests, but that the other side will be prepared to sign up to.

There. That was almost too easy. Maybe a lumberjack would have been more of a challenge.

Chapter 7
So is one picture really worth 1,000 words?

A small experiment designed to test the above proposition; a few thoughts – the experiment having proved inconclusive – on the relative strengths and weaknesses of verbal and visual communication; and some observations on how words and pictures work most effectively together.

Maybe the old saying isn't meant to be taken literally. But, in my working life, I come across quite a few people who seem to believe it. So I wonder if you would be prepared to take part in a little experiment?

What I'd like you to do is look, for a few moments, at this picture.

Adorable, aren't they? Now, I'd like you to read the small print overleaf.

Oh my god, these kittens are so cute! To start with, they are very, very small – probably not more than 12 centimetres from nose to tip of tail. And their fur looks so incredibly soft. They have little tiny pink noses, and teeny weeny whiskers, and there's something about the way they are peeking out of the basket that makes you just want to pick them up and squeeze them, although obviously not too hard or they might be crushed to death. I'm trying very hard to think of something else even half as cute, just to give you an idea how cute they are. Baby ducklings, maybe. Have you ever seen a mother duck proudly swimming across with a pond with a line of tiny babies straggling along behind her, paddling furiously to keep up? That's pretty cute, isn't it? But these kittens (oh yes, did I mention that two of them have their little paws up on the side of the basket?) are much, much, much cuter. Actually, it makes me feel quite weepy just thinking about how small and defenceless they are; how easy it would be for a predator – a fierce dog or even a marauding fox – just to snatch one of them in its powerful jaws and crush it with one bite. Funny, that, I've mentioned the possibility of the kittens being crushed to death twice now; I wonder what that proves. It almost suggests that I have a subconscious desire to see tiny, innocent things destroyed. God, I hope not, that would make me a total wacko. But anyway, let's get back to the cuteness of these kittens. Perhaps it would help if we imagined a device called a Cute-ometer, specifically designed for the purpose of quantifying cuteness. Well, if such a thing existed, I'm absolutely certain that these kittens I'm looking at would send the reading right off the top of the scale – it would be a bit like that scene in *Spinal Tap* where the guy says he has special amplifiers built with volume controls that go right up to 11 instead of the usual 10, because he likes to play so loud. The Cute-ometer would need to go up to 11 or even 12 to measure the cuteness of these kittens. Even then, it wouldn't really begin to do justice to just how cute they are. But maybe before we go any further, we should pause a moment to consider what we really mean by 'cute'. Is it the same as 'sweet', for example? Or 'pretty'? Or 'adorable'? I think, for me, the word has a meaning of its own that nothing else really captures; to do with the response that the 'possessor' of cuteness evokes in others. I think it's very basic, actually; to do with the protective instinct that impels us to care for our young. When we see something cute, we go 'aaaaah!'; our pupils dilate; and we're ready, if necessary, to assume a nurturing role. I know I would with these kittens. I'd be happy to let them live in my bedroom, and I'd make a bed for them out of one my old jumpers. And if anything tried to attack them – that mean old fox I mentioned earlier, for example – I'd kill it with my bare hands. I would. Well, maybe not with my bare hands. I'd probably use a stick. Just whack it a few times on the head, or break its spine maybe. Until I was absolutely sure that the kittens were no longer under any threat. You see, I think that's the effect that extreme cuteness has on most people. It makes us want to kill things. Or maybe that's just me. Anyway, putting such philosophical abstractions aside for the time being, let's return to the cuteness of these kittens – which I feel I haven't yet really succeeded in conveying adequately. Maybe poetry would help; after all, it tends to be more effective than prose in communicating intense emotional experience. So, let's see ... not feeling very inspired, actually ... perhaps something like, 'Little kittens, little kittens, I adore you so/Because you're very small and cute/And always on the go/Poking your little pink noses into everything/ Wherever you may go.' Hmm, not very successful. I don't know what even made me think it was worth trying to write poetry. I've never been any good at it. I just don't have that kind of creative ability. A talentless hack, that's me. Just a plain journeyman wordsmith. Functional prose, that's what I'm good at. To describe how cute these kittens are – to really bring their cuteness alive for the reader – you'd need the sublime poetic gifts of a Shelley or a Keats. One of those guys. Actually, it's made me rather depressed thinking about it: the recognition of my own inability to do anything like justice to the cuteness of those kittens. I call myself a professional writer, and yet – confronted by their extreme cuteness – words simply fail me. It makes me feel that maybe I should be thinking about a career change. Do something better suited to my very limited abilities. Become a traffic warden, maybe, or a tree surgeon (although that wouldn't be much good because I'm afraid of heights). Or retrain as a primary school teacher; I've always rather fancied the idea of teaching young kids ... Hmm, yes, I think I'll look into it. I really think that might be the career for me – although my name might be a problem. Mr Camp. I think the kids would probably give me a pretty hard time about that. Might have to think about changing my name if I'm really serious about becoming a teacher. Funny, really. It looks as if the cuteness of these kittens might have changed my whole life – by helping me to understand my limitations as a writer, and find my true vocation. They really are *so* cute.

So, which conveyed to you more successfully the cuteness of those kittens: one small picture or 1,000 words? (Count them by the way, if you want to check the methodology of this experiment.)

Yes, I thought you might say that. And even as a writer, I can't deny that a visual image is better suited to communicating cuteness than any number of words. But, on the other hand, consider this:

These kittens are six weeks old.

It would take an awful lot of pictures to get that idea across. In fact, it would be virtually impossible. The obvious conclusion: like knives and forks, words and pictures are good at doing different things. Communicating cuteness, as our experiment has proved, is one of the things that pictures do better than words. And, of course, it's generally true that images are a more effective way of instantly conveying moods and emotions, as well as physical appearances.

What are words good at? A fairly random list of things that are much easier to do verbally than visually might include:

- presenting arguments
- imparting information
- listing cake ingredients
- making excuses
- explaining complex ideas

- explaining simple ideas
- differentiating between two similar things
- analysing emotional states
- insulting people
- most kinds of non-slapstick humour
- conveying how something smells
- critiquing
- summarising events
- informing your partner what it is about him/her that drives you nuts

... well, you get the idea (though, of course, you wouldn't if I'd attempted to convey it visually). But I hope I haven't given you the impression that I want to stir up some kind of war between words and pictures. All I am attempting to do is redress the balance a bit, in a world where the visual seems to have gained the upper hand over the verbal. I'm a passionate believer in the power of words, but I'm not a fundamentalist. I'm perfectly happy to attend the odd service at the Church of the Sacred Image, from time to time. (I tend, for example, to send photos of my kids to their grandparents, rather than writing lengthy descriptions of how much they have grown.)

And anyway, in my professional life at least, there's no need to take sides. In fact, it would be disastrous if I did, since nearly all the communications I'm asked to write combine words and images.

How do words and images work best together? There's a whole book to be written in reply to that question, but

this isn't it. I'm just going to make a few general observations on the subject, the first of which concerns:

The wrong way to use words and images together

This is easy. The wrong way is to use words and images
that merely duplicate each other – as, for example, would
be the case if I wrote 'Three cute kittens' under a picture
of three cute kittens. The words would be serving no
purpose but to tell the viewer/reader something that the
picture had already successfully communicated.

Perhaps that doesn't sound like too serious a problem. So
what, if the visual and verbal elements in a piece of
communication cover the same ground? Where's the
harm in a bit of repetition?

To answer that, let's briefly consider an ad you may have
seen fairly recently. We're looking at a bottle of beer with
the cap removed and replaced upside down, so that it
looks as if the bottle is wearing a crown. Over this, the
headline reads: 'King of beers'.

One problem, of course, is that the beer in question is a
disgustingly watery American brew, so the claim is breathtakingly untrue. But, from our point of view, a much worse
offence is the way the words trample on the picture's toes.

The bottle top crown is a moderately inventive visual pun
– which, taken alone, might well give the viewer a small

'reward'; the pleasurable feeling of having successfully decoded a lightly concealed meaning. With the plonky headline gormlessly spelling it out – nudging the reader in the ribs and saying 'geddit?' – the pleasure is dramatically reduced, perhaps lost altogether.

So that's why, in persuasive communication, words and pictures shouldn't ever simply duplicate each other's function: because it may well make the desired response, and therefore the intended result, a bit less likely.

The right way to use words and images together

You can probably guess what I'm going to say. Exactly. The right way is to use words and images to complement each other, so that each does the job that it is good at – as, for example, would be the case if I wrote 'These kittens are six weeks old' under a picture of three cute kittens.

But, again, there's a bit more to it than that. In the very best persuasive communication, words and images don't just sit comfortably alongside each other, like contented flatmates; they shack up together and enjoy a pretty intense relationship.

Let's look at a few examples. Here, just along the road from my house, is a poster which reads: 'Had the day from hell? Taste the chip from heaven.' Between the first sentence and the second, there is a picture of – you guessed it, an enormous golden chip. This image adds nothing to the meaning of the words: we can perfectly well remove it, and the headline still makes perfect sense. But, unlike 'king of beers', the giant chip does contribute something to the success of the communication – appetite appeal. Merely describing this crinkle cut baton of reconstituted potato mush as 'the chip from heaven' doesn't make us salivate; the photo – if we're very, very hungry – may.

Still on the fast-food theme, there's another ad on the bus shelter at the end of my road, introducing us to: 'XYZ, the enormously satisfying new pizza.' It's illustrated by a digitally enhanced photograph of a young man with an exaggeratedly wide mouth, opened slightly to reveal disturbing numbers of sharp little teeth. It's definitely creepy, but I suppose it's intended to give a bit of a twist to the rather dull headline: a generic claim ('enormously satisfying') is made engaging by an element of slightly surreal visual hyperbole. We might say that, rather than simply illustrating the headline, the picture comments upon the words ('When we say enormously satisfying, we mean big enough to choke a Ghoulish Mutant Teenager to death!')

Or what about this, in today's paper: an ad for a new credit card. The headline reads: 'The new XYZ card. What's stopping you?' We see a man being sat upon by an elephant. Broadly, this works in the same way as the pizza ad – through surreal exaggeration – but it seems a bit more successful, because there is at least a little wit in this communication. The image itself is mildly amusing. But, more important, there is a small 'reward' to be had from decoding the combined meaning of words and picture: that only a circumstance as bizarre as being pinioned by a pachyderm can possibly account for anyone failing to apply for this particular piece of plastic.

But we still haven't found what we are looking for; an example of words and pictures achieving complete can't-live-without-each-other interdependence. Ah yes, we have now. Rummaging around in my office, I unearth an award-winning ad for a well-known children's charity. A baby, wearing nothing but a nappy, sits alone in a dark alley. He's holding a syringe, which he appears to be on the point of plunging into his arm. The headline reads: 'John Donaldson. Aged 25.' It's perfect. The image, taken alone, is shocking, but meaningless: why would a baby inject itself with heroin? How, for that matter, would a baby inject itself with heroin? The headline, read in isolation, is a bald factual statement. But, in collision with each other, the two elements compel us to think; to formulate, and then consider, the proposition that childhood deprivation leads to adult degradation.

Of course, you may reject this proposition. And, in any case, you may not share my admiration for this particular ad. But it doesn't matter. I have drawn it to your attention only to demonstrate the highest form of union between words and pictures in persuasive communication; the kind where neither makes any sense without the other.

Chapter 8
Working with writers

A frankly somewhat specialised chapter, relevant to you only if your working life ever brings you into contact with professional persuasive writers. No? Then please feel free to skip the next 10 pages.

I hope that reading this book will help you to become a better persuasive writer, and that this will be especially useful to you in your working life. But there may, nevertheless, be occasions when you will need to call in a professional to work with you on a piece of persuasive communication. So I thought it might be helpful to give you a few suggestions about how you can get the best out of these talented, but sometimes temperamental creatures.

Of course, the most important, and hardest, part of the process is finding the right person. And I'm afraid there's not much I can say to make it any easier. One practical problem is that there are so many different kinds of writer out there. Depending on the nature of the project, you might need an advertising copywriter, a corporate journalist, a communications strategist, a technical author, an information architect, a scriptwriter, a speechwriter, a web content deviser, or even a word-carpenter. (OK, I made the last one up, but all the others really exist.)

A much bigger problem, though, once you have decided on the appropriate sub-species, is finding the right individual. Why's it so hard? Because, frankly, there is an awful lot of dross to sift through. There are thousands of people around the country offering their services as professional writers. And while I have no wish to cast any sort of slur on my chosen profession, I'm afraid you will find the vast majority of these to be slack-jawed cretins and semi-literate charlatans; a feckless rabble of drunk-ards, shysters and con artists, barely able – even when sober – to tell an active verb from an aardvark.

Well, maybe I exaggerate – but only slightly. My advice? Take time over choosing a writer to work with, and be ruthless. It's important not to rush the selection process for the blindingly obvious reason that you need to read a reasonable amount of a writer's work to find out if he's any good. A lot of writers can write the odd snappy headline, but totally lack the ability to hold the reader's attention for more than a couple of paragraphs.

The ruthlessness is self-explanatory, I think. You wouldn't eat at a restaurant where the food was no better than you could cook yourself at home – so why employ a writer who doesn't use words better than you? Apply what you have learned from this book. Ask yourself if what you are reading reflects an understanding of the 3 Rs of good persuasive writing. Has every word been chosen with care, to engage with this specific reader, and to elicit a response which makes the desired result more likely? You may not feel your own persuasive writing skills are highly developed yet, but be confident in your ability to judge other people's. I think you know enough to recognise good writing when you see it.

So, having disposed of that pretty briskly, let's move on to the working relationship between you and your chosen writer. Again, there is a huge amount that I could say, based on hundreds of happy and not-so-happy relationships I've had with clients over the years. But instead, I'm going to keep it fairly brief by focusing on ...

The five worst things you can say to a writer

Which are:

1 'Have you ever worked in the premoulded polymerised thermal closures sector before?'

A great way to get the relationship with your writer off on the wrong foot. Of course, it may seem perfectly reasonable to you to enquire whether he has experience in your particular field.

But, actually, it's like a theatre director asking an actor whether he has ever played the Third Gentleman in *Titus Andronicus*. If he has talent and technique, he'll inhabit the role successfully. If he hasn't – well, it won't make the slightest difference whether he's tackled the part before. He'll still be rubbish.

The skill of a good persuasive writer is to understand the story that needs to be told, and find a way of making it engaging to the particular reader who is being addressed. Certainly, a bit of background knowledge and a firm grasp of the specific issues are essential. But these can relatively quickly be acquired. Just as with the actor, though, it's talent and technique that count.

I'd go further. Good writers tend to have lively, enquiring (not to say dilettante) minds. They enjoy soaking up information and are stimulated by new subjects. So it may very well be that they do their best work when they are in territory that is not over-familiar; and, conversely, that even an excellent writer can get a little jaded when he feels that he knows the ground he is covering rather too well.

In fact, writing this, I'm suddenly struck by the perfect answer to the above question: 'No, never. That's exactly why I'd like to.'

2 'We've written it ourselves – all it needs is a bit of a polish.'

By far the most depressing thing about being a professional writer is the fact that everybody thinks they can do your job. And what makes it so much worse is that it's true, they can ... up to a point. It's not like being a neurosurgeon or a ballet dancer or even a satellite dish installer; trades where a high degree of specialist expertise and skill acts as an insurmountable barrier to entry. Everyone I work for can, to a greater or lesser extent, do what I do for a living: tap at a keyboard and make words appear on a screen.

So this brings us back to the point I was making in the restaurant analogy I served up a couple of paragraphs ago: if you want to get the best from a writer, you need to believe – and behave as if you believe – that he has expertise and skills you lack. Equally important, you need to understand what these are.

If you do (and I hope you do by now), you'll knowing that bringing in a professional to 'polish' an existing piece of writing is an almost entirely pointless exercise, like building your own bridge, then getting Isambard Kingdom Brunel to apply a couple of coats of Dulux Weathershield. All the important decisions – about how to engage the reader, what the argument and structure should be, where the emphasis should fall, how much supporting evidence is needed – have already been made. Unless the writer rips it up and starts again, it's too late to do anything but tidy up the punctuation and get rid of the odd clunky phrase.

3 'We've tweaked the opening sentence, cut the second and third paras, and added a bit about our commitment to customer service … but otherwise, it's exactly what you wrote.'
A good piece of writing isn't just a collection of sentences, it's the expression of a single, coherent thought process. This doesn't mean, of course, that it is somehow sacrosanct; that it can't be cut or expanded; that the emphasis

can't be shifted; or that adjustments can't be made to the tone. But it does mean that tinkering with it can be very risky indeed. Even making very small changes to a piece of writing – a substituted word here, a deleted phrase there – can seriously damage the flow; cause gaps to appear in the logic, and dramatically weaken the argument; or even turn the intended meaning on its head. One small but clumsy tweak and the whole structure can start to disintegrate, a bit like a jumper unravelling when you tug at a tiny thread.

So, in my view, it's *always* best to let writers make their own revisions. Very occasionally, that may not be possible: a looming print deadline, urgent changes required, and the writer's on holiday in the West Indies (hah!). But, in the vast majority of cases, however tempting it may be to open the document on your PC and go to work on it, you'll get a better finished result if you provide the writer with feedback, then let him make whatever changes are necessary.

4 'Can you make it more punchy?'

You know that feeling when you're suddenly overwhelmed by a desire to smash, batter, grind and pummel the person nearest to you? Well, that's what wells up inside me whenever I hear the 'p' word.

'Punchy', as far as the repellent little word has any meaning, is used to describe a highly emphatic style of writing that barks at the reader. In short, staccato sentences. Like this. Making impressive, but hollow-sounding claims. Not just 100% of the time. But 110%. Every time.

Warm and engaging? Rigorously argued? Intelligent and insightful? No thanks, we'd prefer it punchy.

Putting aside that little bugbear of mine, there's a broader point to be made here about the art of giving a writer useful and positive feedback; the kind that will actually enable him to produce a better piece of persuasive writing.

I'd suggest that, before you make any comment, you should ideally read any piece of writing three times:

Read-through 1 – architecture, not doorknobs

It's important to judge the overall effect of a piece of writing before getting involved in the nuts and bolts of content and style. So first, read straight through from start to finish, without stopping to make notes. Naturally, you should try to put yourself in the reader's shoes. How would what you are reading sound if you were coming to it cold?

Read-through 2 – content, structure, emphasis

On your second reading, you should make a note of anything that is factually inaccurate. More generally, you should assess whether the content of the piece does the necessary job. Has the writer left out anything that you feel the reader needs to know? Or, conversely, is there anything that comes under the heading of 'too much information'?

Also, at this stage, you should consider whether you are happy with the structure and emphasis of the piece. Do the arguments seem to come in the right, logical order? Do you agree with the priority that the writer has given to the various points?

Read-through 3 – tone, phrasing, vocabulary

Finally, read through again, paying attention to the words and phrasing. Is there anything which you feel the reader might stumble over? For example, a word she may not understand – or a phrase that seems inappropriately slangy or over-formal? (If it isn't too embarrassing, it can be a good idea to read aloud at this stage, to give yourself the clearest possible sense of how the piece flows, and how the individual words sound.)

Also, is there anything which you feel should be more clearly expressed? If so, mark the offending word, phrase or sentence – and note what your concern is. Don't make your own revisions, but it's fine to suggest an alternative wording, if you think that would help the writer understand your concern.

Let me show you how that might look:

Read-through 3 – tone, phrasing, vocabulary *(I like the first heading 'architecture, not doorknobs' – can we have something similar here?)*

Finally, read through again, paying attention to the words and phrasing. Is there anything which you feel the reader might stumble over? *(Would 'trip over' be better?)* For example, a word she may not understand – or a phrase that seems inappropriately slangy *(Is there such a word?)* or over-formal? (If it isn't too embarrassing, it can be a good idea to read aloud at this stage, to give yourself the clearest possible sense of how the piece flows, and how the individual words sound.) *(Why should it be embarrassing? Do you mean because people might think you're mad? If so, maybe we need to spell it out.)*

Also, is there anything which you feel should be more clearly expressed? *(Not very keen on sentences starting with 'Also' – sounds a bit like an afterthought)* If so, mark the offending word, phrase or sentence – and note what your concern is. Don't make your own revisions, but it's fine to suggest an alternative wording, if you think that would help the writer understand your concern. *(Fab, Lindsay. Anybody told you what a great writer you are recently?)*

5 'It's wrong to start a sentence with 'and' … '
It isn't, and it never has been, as I think we established earlier. But the point I'm making here is a more general one, to do with (oh dear, this is going to sound toe-curlingly pompous) professional respect.

If you've taken time and trouble over finding a really good writer to work with, trust him. Certainly, you should feel free to question what he has written, even to suggest changes and improvements. But remember that, in persuasive writing, right and wrong are, to a very large extent, a matter of taste and judgement. Exercising these is a very important part of what you are paying a writer to do for you. If you're not prepared to let him, you're not getting value for money.

And he definitely won't enjoy working with you.

I hope I haven't made working with professional writers sound too daunting. That certainly wasn't my intention. But, in case you are still feeling a little uncertain about your ability to establish happy and productive working relationships with members of my profession, I thought it might help to end this chapter by looking very briefly at ...

The three best things you can say to a writer

Which are, of course:

1 'No hurry, take as long as you like.'

2 'Go on – name your price.'

3 'Fancy a drink?'

Section Four

More than words can say

More than words can say

An admission that this book hasn't quite lived up to its original billing; an attempt to show how the three Rs of good persuasive writing can actually be applied to all forms of communication, verbal and non-verbal; and some thoughts about how understanding the principles of persuasive communication might help you in your most important relationships.

And so we approach the end of this journey. I hope that it hasn't seemed as long to you as it has to me; and that, in return for the time you've invested, you feel you've gained something that may be of value to you. But, before we finally reach our destination, exchange firm handshakes and go our separate ways, I'd like to leave you with a couple more things to think about.

Persuasive writing? Not necessarily

The first – and you may have spotted this for yourself – is that this isn't really a book about persuasive writing. Well it is, obviously, but only in part. My real subject is broader than that. With the exception of the bits about things like punctuation and paragraphs, nearly everything I've said here can be applied equally well to most forms of verbal communication – from being interviewed by John Humphrys on the *Today* programme to chatting on the phone with a prospective client. All you need to do is delete the words 'the reader', which I have used hundreds of times, and substitute something like 'the listener', 'the audience' or even just 'the other person'.

I don't feel too badly about having fudged this issue slightly. My specific expertise is as a writer of printed (or on-screen) communications, so I've naturally focused on the written-to-be-read word. And, in any case, I'm sure you've been able to see this bigger picture for yourself. It's no great leap to recognise that, if the written words you use matter a lot, so do the ones that come out of your mouth.

But I'd like to go one step further, by pointing out that the most important principle I've talked about in this book can be applied to all forms of persuasive communication, non-verbal as well as verbal. That principle, of course, is RRR: in virtually any situation, I would suggest, it pays to remember who your 'reader' is, and what result you are hoping to achieve.

That big job interview you have coming up. Will wearing your new Homer Simpson tie get you the response you want from your prospective new employer, and a place on the shortlist?

Or, if that seems too brain-paralysingly obvious to be worth saying, allow me to turn the clock back to early 2003, when

I took part in that staggeringly enormous demonstration against the Iraq war. I'm glad I did. But, even at the time, I had serious doubts about the effectiveness of such an event as an exercise in persuasive communication. We chanted, we sang, we shuffled very slowly along Piccadilly. We rushed home and watched ourselves on the news. It was an unforgettable day. But it didn't stop the war.

Did we expect it to? Was that the result we were aiming to achieve? If so, who was the 'reader' we were addressing? And what response were we trying to elicit, in order to make the intended result more likely?

I'm only asking. Speaking for myself, I knew that the war would go ahead, and that nothing that two million (or just under 500, if you believed police estimates) of us did on the bitterly cold streets of central London that day would make the slightest difference. If anything, TV pictures of some marchers holding aloft pictures of Saddam and defacing American flags may have stiffened the warrior resolve of our political leaders.

I marched that day because I was angry and frustrated, and wanted to express those feelings. But if any of my fellow marchers believed that what they were doing had a chance of changing minds in Downing Street and the White House, they were always going to be disappointed. Was there anything else we could have done which would have been more effective? I don't think so. But that's beside the point, which is that, assuming the intended result was to prevent Iraq being invaded, the demonstration failed – and was always going to fail – as a piece of persuasive communication.

Applying the RRR principle to personal relationships

At the risk of sounding a bit flaky, I want to finish by taking this argument another step further; by suggesting – ever so tentatively – that the principles we've been talking about here can also usefully be applied to the most important relationships in your life.

I'm thinking, for example, of a friend of mine whose wife used to work ridiculously long hours. Every evening at about 7.30, when she still wasn't home and the children were trampolining on the sofa or starting small fires in the understairs cupboard, he'd begin to feel a bit depressed. And by the time she did get back, usually quite a bit later, he was thoroughly miserable.

Being a thoughtful and intelligent sort of fellow, my friend decided that, if he wanted his wife to come home earlier, the best approach was to be as unpleasant to her as possible when she was late. Biting sarcasm and spiteful remarks would, he felt sure, achieve the desired result.

Oddly enough, they didn't. His wife started to come home even later. So my friend had another idea: he'd give her the silent treatment. When she came in late, he'd be engrossed in the newspaper, and wouldn't even bother to put it down.

That didn't work either. But then, this friend of mine hit upon a radical notion: he decided to try being nice to his wife when she came home late. In fact, the later she was, the nicer he'd be. He'd bring her a glass of wine, ask her about her day, maybe even have supper ready for her.

The result? I'm afraid I can't answer that. I wouldn't, after all, want to intrude upon the intimate details of my friend's relationship with his wife – though I will say they seem a lot happier together these days. But, from a persuasive communication standpoint, it seems to me he finally got it right: his best chance of achieving the result he wanted was to understand that she was hardly likely to rush home, leaving urgent work unfinished, if she knew that bitterness and recriminations – rather than a tasty hotpot – awaited her there.

Why the way we talk to ourselves matters very much indeed

I am, as I think I may have mentioned, quite keen on tennis. So much so, that a few years ago I started playing in local tournaments. Occasionally, I would find myself matched with another slighly overweight, sweaty middle-aged bloke, with a large mortgage and a dodgy back-hand. But, more often, my opponents were several decades younger than me, a zillion times fitter – oh yes, and much, much better at tennis.

So I used to lose a lot. But not as much as you might imagine. On a number of occasions, I won matches that

I clearly should have lost, and these reversals of the form-book always followed the same pattern. Early on in the match, my opponent would miss what he considered to be an easy shot, and start cursing himself. 'You are so crap!' he'd say. And from that point on, every time things went against him – whether or not through his own incompetence – the torrent of verbal self-abuse would flow more freely. ('You're playing like a moron!' 'What was that supposed to be?' 'You're just giving points away!' and much more in the same vein.)

Presumably, in these situations, my young opponents were trying to talk themselves into playing better. But it hardly ever worked. In fact, it almost always had the opposite effect. As soon as I heard 'You are such complete crap!' from the other side of the net, I knew I was probably going to pull off another implausible victory.

It's an extreme example of the way in which the words people use when talking to themselves can influence their behaviour, and the results they achieve. But I want to suggest that, to some extent, the same thing can happen for all of us, every day of our lives. From the dawning of consciousness in early childhood, whenever we are awake we are conducting an almost continuous dialogue with ourselves, usually inside our heads though occasionally aloud. Much of it, of course, is inconsequential chatter ('Six o'clock? Mm, time for a beer ...'), but some of what we say to ourselves can have an impact on the things that matter most to us.

I mean the things we tell ourselves when we're facing any kind of decision in our lives ('Look before you leap'); when we're wondering if we're capable of doing something we've never done before ('No point even trying'); or when we've had an idea, and we're not sure if it's any good ('It's rubbish, like everything you ever think of').

Of course, our 'inner critic', as my friends in psychotherapeutic circles refer to this insistent little voice, isn't necessarily our enemy. If we tell ourselves, for example, that what we've done in our work isn't good enough, it may well spur us on to do better. Without healthy self-criticism, no poem would ever go beyond its first draft; no prototype would ever be developed and refined; no athlete would ever beat his own personal best.

But I suspect that for most of us, most of the time – or, at least, for many of us, much of the time – the things we say to ourselves have a predominantly negative effect. We tend to talk ourselves out of, rather than into, being as creative, open-minded, engaged, friendly, funny, positive and loving as we have the potential to be. We persuade ourselves to be less than we could be.

What can we do about it? That's hard. If I'm right that, like me, you have a consistently critical little voice inside your head, always ready to remind you why you shouldn't take a risk, how you failed last time, what you stand to lose if things turn out badly ... well, it isn't going to be easily silenced. That voice has developed its distinctive tone, and the repetitive script it recites, over many, many years.

In my case, I'm pretty sure it's with me for life. But I do believe it's possible to listen to that voice, consider what it says, and choose to disregard it. I think we can learn answer back. I think, at the very least, we can make some significant revisions to the constant stream of persuasive communications we direct at ourselves:

'No point even trying ... '
> Might as well give it a shot ...

'Another of your rubbish ideas ... '
> Hmm, could be interesting ...

'You are so crap!'
> No, actually, I'm doing the best I
> can ... and guess what, I'm enjoying myself.

So here we are fast approaching the final page, and it's looking very much as if I may have misled you. Because, having started so unassumingly, this little book seems to have undergone something of a transformation. Having promised you, in the opening chapter, no more than a bit of help with developing your writing skills, I find myself ending with a very big claim indeed: that understanding the principles involved in good persuasive communication could help you interact more successfully with the outside world and build happier, more productive relationships with other people, as well as with yourself. In short, *Can I Change Your Mind?* has failed to do exactly what it says on the tin.

Damn. All I can say in my defence is that when we set out, I wasn't expecting to end up here. 'Why do I write?' asked the historian AJP Taylor. 'Because how else would I find out what I think?' Writing this book has helped me to find out what I think; to know a bit better who I am; and to understand why my strongest belief is in the power of words.

If just a bit of that belief has rubbed off on you, my reader, then I've achieved the result I wanted.

PS ...

Think of the following pieces as the bonus tracks at the end of the CD; the rare live recording; the previously unreleased acoustic version; the out-takes swept up from the studio floor.

Or, less metaphorically, you could regard this last thin sliver of the book as a few odds and ends that didn't quite fit anywhere else, but which may be of interest to the more enthusiastic student of persuasive writing.

If that describes you, don't miss the opportunity to find out whether you've learned anything, right at the very end.

PS ...

What really good persuasive writing looks like

Unless you work in advertising or marketing, you've probably never heard of Jeremy Bullmore. Who is he? A hugely respected advertising man who, since retiring from full-time agency life a decade or so ago, has become a revered commentator on the business of marketing and communications.

More to the point here, though, Jeremy Bullmore is the finest persuasive writer who walks the earth. His ability to win a reader over to his point of view verges on the supernatural. Read just a couple of paragraphs of his writing and you find yourself unable to imagine ever disagreeing with him about anything. If those nutcases who believe that George Bush and the Duke of Edinburgh are really extra-terrestrial giant lizards bent on world domination were to hire Jeremy to write their recruitment literature, I'd join them tomorrow.

So I think you'll understand why I felt it would be criminal to deprive you of the opportunity to become acquainted with The Master. I chose the following piece almost at random. It comes from the agony column which Jeremy writes in the advertising industry weekly, *Campaign*.

Q A distant relation is interested in advertising and has asked me for help. In all honesty, given your time again, would you choose this industry above all else, and if so, what would be the chief reason?

In all honesty, I probably wouldn't. 'Given your time again' is a beguiling beacon of a phrase. It lures you into a wonderland in which you can apply the knowledge you've acquired over the years to a reinstated innocence. Real life doesn't let you do this.

So I expect I'd think about being a world-famous saxophonist or portrait painter or geologist: while being happily ignorant of all the vexations that must surely plague even the most successful saxophonists, portrait painters or geologists.

When you compare a world you know with a world you don't know, the world you know is likely to come off badly. So, given my time again, I'd probably not choose advertising.

Yet I can't, off-hand, think of any other trade that would pay me to think about all the things I'd want to think about anyway: about markets and economies and business and people and communications and choice and freedom and words and pictures and new technologies and competitive persuasion and the nature of progress and Toilet Duck and Sunny D and how to see through the eyes of others. I can't, off-hand, think of any other legitimate trade that is

less deferential, less snobby, less conventionally respect-
able or more fun.

So, given my time again, I'd probably not choose
advertising. But I'm pretty sure that I'd live to regret it.

Originally, I was planning to deconstruct this piece for
you; to go through it line by line, pointing out masterly
uses of irony and understatement, and how the repetition
of 'and' makes that long, long sentence utterly irresistible.

But, on reflection, I think Jeremy's writing speaks for
itself. For much more of the same, read *Behind the Scenes
in Advertising* published by the World Advertising
Research Centre; or his most recent book, *Apples, Insights
and Mad Inventors*, published by Wiley.

PPS ...

(Impertinent comments by Lindsay Camp)

1 Never use a metaphor, simile or other figure of speech which you are used to seeing in print.
Yup, couldn't agree more: see pages 133–5.

2 Never use a long word where a short one will do.
Check. See page 142.

3 If it is possible to cut a word out, cut it out.
Hmm. Not sure about this, George. Yes, it's generally agreed that good writing doesn't waste a word, but it rather depends on how you define waste. In any piece of writing, there are words – and sentences, and even paragraphs – that could be cut without destroying the sense of the piece. For example, descriptive adjectives are rarely strictly necessary, and the same can be said of humorous remarks. (Oh yes, and anything that appears in brackets.) But, of course, when you make cuts, you often lose something that may be of value to your reader – rhythm, flow, colour, personality.

And by the way: 'If it is possible to cut a word ~~out~~, cut it ~~out~~.'

4 Never use the passive voice where you can use the active.

OK. I suppose. Every guide to good writing always says this, so I guess there must be something in it. But is the reader's understanding or enjoyment really affected whenever the passive voice is used? I'm assailed by doubt.

5 Never use a foreign phrase, a scientific word or a jargon word if you can think of an everyday English equivalent.

Bien sûr, George. Every time a writer uses a foreign phrase, scientific or jargon word, it fills me with *Weltschmerz*.

6 Break any of these rules sooner than say anything outright barbarous.

'Outright barbarous' – I love that. You're the man, George.

PPPS ...

Go on, brief yourself

Next time you have something difficult to write, you might like to try writing yourself a brief before you start. The following headings are loosely based on the kind of briefing forms widely used in the persuasive communications business. You may find them helpful ...

Reason (*Why are you doing this?*)
What's the background to the piece of writing you're planning? What, very broadly, is its purpose? At this stage, it may even be worth questioning whether it's right to write: might a phone call or face-to-face chat be a better option?

Result (*What, specifically, are you trying to achieve?*)
What do you want to happen as a direct result of this piece of writing? It's OK to have secondary objectives, but be absolutely clear what the most important one is. If you're uncertain about this, ask yourself how you'll know whether this communication has succeeded or failed.

Reader (*Who is she, and what's she like?*)
What do you know about the person (or type of person) you're writing for? What can you reasonably assume? What can you intelligently guess? Remember that building up a useful picture of your reader involves empathy as well as logic.

Reader's state of mind *(What does she think/feel now?)*
Now you need to zero in on what your reader thinks and/or feels about the matter in hand – before she reads whatever you are planning to write. How interested is she in the subject you are about to raise? How knowledgeable? What is her attitude likely to be?

Response *(What do you want her to think/feel?)*
What, bearing in mind her current state of mind, could you realistically hope to leave your reader thinking/ feeling – after she has read what you are about to write? This is where you need to define the response which, you believe, is most likely to lead to the result you want.

Competitive promise *(What's going to change her mind?)*
What's your single strongest claim or argument – the core thought that you hope will take your reader on the journey from what she thought/felt before reading to what you want her to think/feel after reading? What is it that makes whatever you are 'selling' different or special? Remember, it's unlikely this will be based exclusively on measurable facts; in most cases, it will probably combine rational and emotive elements.

Support *(Why should she believe you?)*
Finally, make a note of all the good reasons why your reader should believe what you are promising. You may or may not include this information in the finished piece of writing, but it's important that, if pressed, you should be able make your claims stand up. If not, your competitive promise almost certainly won't sound believable.

PPPPS ...

A few things to do

It's all right, you don't have to read this. No, really, it's optional. In fact, it shouldn't really be here at all – given all my earlier protestations about how this isn't intended to be a 'teach yourself persuasive writing' manual.

But, since you've been kind enough to stick with me to the bitter end, I feel it might look ungenerous if I didn't at least offer you the opportunity to find out whether you've learned anything. So here are a few little persuasive writing exercises.

Remember, if you do have a crack at any of the following, there are no correct answers.

1 That Lonely Hearts ad
Yes, I know you're in a happy long-term relationship. But imagine if you weren't. Write a Lonely Hearts ad – 50 words max – that would leave your perfect partner no option but to respond. (OK, if you insist, you can pretend you haven't yet met your actual real life partner, and use him/her as your 'target' reader.)

It might be a good idea to go back and look at pages 65–68 before you start.

2 Job description

Write a brief description of your job (or, if you don't have one, what you spend your day doing) that would make sense to an intelligent six-year-old.

Then do the same for a reader who does similar work to yours in a different organisation.

3 Skip this

We're doing some renovation work, so we have a skip outside our house. Every night, people come and dump old mattresses and TV sets in it. It cost £150, so I feel rather bitter about this.

But I've had an idea. I'm planning to fasten a notice to the skip that will persuade people not to put their rubbish in it. I wonder if you would be kind enough to write it for me?

4 Rewrite the Mission Statement

Does the company or organisation you work for have a Mission Statement? If so, is it any good? Thought not. Rewrite it, bearing in mind who you think the most important reader is and what result you are trying to achieve.

5 'Never knowingly undersold'

It's one of the great all-time slogans. And what makes it so brilliant is the compression; three words that express a compelling and surprisingly complex thought.

But maybe it's starting to sound just a little dated. In fact, I wonder if a younger generation of John Lewis shoppers even know exactly what it means?

Your task, then, is to update it. But there are two rules you must obey:

1 Your version must convey the same meaning.
2 Your version must not use any of the same words.

I'm sure you can do better than this:

> We'll never charge you more than you'd pay in another shop, provided we're aware of the fact that the other shop is selling the same item for less.

6 For 'compact' read 'too small to swing a gerbil'
As I think I mentioned earlier, estate agents are serial abusers of the English language. Write a short classified ad for your present home without lapsing into estate-agent-speak. If the kitchen is tiny, why not try admitting it? Being honest might help you find a buyer. 100 words maximum.

7 Job application haikus
Apply for a job in the form of a haiku (a poem of three lines with five, seven and five syllables).

How will doing this make you a better persuasive writer? Hmm, something to do with learning to make every syllable count, I think. Here's one I made earlier:

Chop, chop, chop, chop, chop.

I'd make a good lumberjack.

I've got my own axe.

8. Writing at XYZ College

The following is a genuine excerpt from the prospectus of a well-known college offering courses in media-related subjects. Read it; try to make sense of what it's actually saying; and then write your own version – bearing in mind that your reader is a young person with an interest in words, communication and the media.

My version is overleaf, but don't look at it until you've written yours.

Writing at XYZ College is distinctive in its approach to writing because it enables students to position themselves as writers within changing environments and technologies and to develop an autonomous practice which will be sustainable because it is responsive to change. Maintaining a common focus on contemporary contexts for writing and on wider issues of cultural and critical concern, Writing at XYZ College offers a flexible learning environment for writing that gives students an extended range of choices and directions for their individual writing practices within a framework of compositional, analytical and contextual enquiry.

Writing at XYZ College is a course designed to help students learn how to make a living as professional writers in the modern world.

The course aims to balance the creative with the commercial – helping students to find their own voice as writers, but also focusing on the rapidly changing marketplace and the many different media in which writers today can practise their craft.

9 Reading exercise

This one is simple. Just read something – anything really, as long as it consists of words and sentences. Then read something else, preferably something better written than the first thing you read. Repeat the exercise tomorrow. And the day after that. And then every day for the rest of your life.

Sorry if this exercise sounds a bit of a chore; but you'll never be a really good writer – persuasive or otherwise – unless you make time for it.

10 Cliché cricket

Finally, a game for two to play on a long motorway journey.

Take it in turns to bat. The player batting reads aloud the slogans on all commercial vehicles on the same carriageway.

Runs are scored if a slogan contains any of the following words:

• Quality	5 runs
• Innovation	10 runs
• Passion/passionate	15 runs
• Deliver/delivering	20 runs
• Driven by	25 runs
• Solutions	30 runs

Slogans may contain more than one scoring word: for example, 'Driven by our passion for delivering quality solutions' would add up to 75 runs.

The batsman is out and his innings ends if 10 successive slogans contain no scoring words.

WWW.CANICHANGEYOURMIND.CO.UK

Any comments, queries or quibbles about anything you've just read? Then I'd be very happy to hear from you, via the website. Go on, drop me a line.

Index

Photo credit

p. 197 kittens copyright © Tony Campbell, 2004